Maurice Ravel

Titles in the series Critical Lives present the work of leading cultural figures of the modern period. Each book explores the life of the artist, writer, philosopher or architect in question and relates it to their major works.

In the same series

Hannah Arendt *Samantha Rose Hill*
Antonin Artaud *David A. Shafer*
John Ashbery *Jess Cotton*
Roland Barthes *Andy Stafford*
Georges Bataille *Stuart Kendall*
Charles Baudelaire *Rosemary Lloyd*
Jean Baudrillard *Emmanuelle Fantin and Bran Nicol*
Simone de Beauvoir *Ursula Tidd*
Samuel Beckett *Andrew Gibson*
Walter Benjamin *Esther Leslie*
John Berger *Andy Merrifield*
Leonard Bernstein *Paul R. Laird*
Joseph Beuys *Claudia Mesch*
Jorge Luis Borges *Jason Wilson*
Constantin Brancusi *Sanda Miller*
Bertolt Brecht *Philip Glahn*
Charles Bukowski *David Stephen Calonne*
Mikhail Bulgakov *J.A.E. Curtis*
William S. Burroughs *Phil Baker*
Byron *David Ellis*
John Cage *Rob Haskins*
Albert Camus *Edward J. Hughes*
Fidel Castro *Nick Caistor*
Paul Cézanne *Jon Kear*
Coco Chanel *Linda Simon*
Noam Chomsky *Wolfgang B. Sperlich*
Jean Cocteau *James S. Williams*
Joseph Conrad *Robert Hampson*
H.D. (Hilda Doolittle) *Lara Vetter*
Salvador Dalí *Mary Ann Caws*
Charles Darwin *J. David Archibald*
Guy Debord *Andy Merrifield*
Claude Debussy *David J. Code*
Gilles Deleuze *Frida Beckman*
Fyodor Dostoevsky *Robert Bird*
Marcel Duchamp *Caroline Cros*
Sergei Eisenstein *Mike O'Mahony*
Frantz Fanon *James S. Williams*
William Faulkner *Kirk Curnutt*
Gustave Flaubert *Anne Green*
Ford Madox Ford *Max Saunders*
Michel Foucault *David Macey*
Benjamin Franklin *Kevin J. Hayes*
Sigmund Freud *Matthew ffytche*
Mahatma Gandhi *Douglas Allen*
Antoni Gaudí *Michael Eaude*
Jean Genet *Stephen Barber*
Allen Ginsberg *Steve Finbow*
Johann Wolfgang von Goethe *Jeremy Adler*
Günter Grass *Julian Preece*
Ernest Hemingway *Verna Kale*
E.T.A. Hoffmann *Ritchie Robertson*
Langston Hughes *W. Jason Miller*
Victor Hugo *Bradley Stephens*
Zora Neale Hurston *Cheryl R. Hopson*
Aldous Huxley *Jake Poller*
J.-K. Huysmans *Ruth Antosh*
Christopher Isherwood *Jake Poller*
Derek Jarman *Michael Charlesworth*
Alfred Jarry *Jill Fell*
James Joyce *Andrew Gibson*
Carl Jung *Paul Bishop*
Franz Kafka *Sander L. Gilman*

Frida Kahlo *Gannit Ankori*
Søren Kierkegaard *Alastair Hannay*
Yves Klein *Nuit Banai*
Arthur Koestler *Edward Saunders*
Akira Kurosawa *Peter Wild*
D. H. Lawrence *David Ellis*
Lenin *Lars T. Lih*
Jack London *Kenneth K. Brandt*
Pierre Loti *Richard M. Berrong*
Rosa Luxemburg *Dana Mills*
Jean-François Lyotard *Kiff Bamford*
René Magritte *Patricia Allmer*
Gustav Mahler *Stephen Downes*
Stéphane Mallarmé *Roger Pearson*
Thomas Mann *Herbert Lehnert and Eva Wessell*
Gabriel García Márquez *Stephen M. Hart*
Karl Marx *Paul Thomas*
Henri Matisse *Kathryn Brown*
Guy de Maupassant *Christopher Lloyd*
Herman Melville *Kevin J. Hayes*
Henry Miller *David Stephen Calonne*
Yukio Mishima *Damian Flanagan*
Eadweard Muybridge *Marta Braun*
Vladimir Nabokov *Barbara Wyllie*
Pablo Neruda *Dominic Moran*
Friedrich Nietzsche *Ritchie Robertson*
Georgia O'Keeffe *Nancy J. Scott*
Richard Owen *Patrick Armstrong*
Octavio Paz *Nick Caistor*
Fernando Pessoa *Bartholomew Ryan*
Pablo Picasso *Mary Ann Caws*
Edgar Allan Poe *Kevin J. Hayes*
Ezra Pound *Alec Marsh*
Sergei Prokofiev *Christina Guillaumier*
Marcel Proust *Adam Watt*
Sergei Rachmaninoff *Rebecca Mitchell*
Maurice Ravel *Emily Kilpatrick*
Arthur Rimbaud *Seth Whidden*
John Ruskin *Andrew Ballantyne*
Jean-Paul Sartre *Andrew Leak*
Erik Satie *Mary E. Davis*
Arnold Schoenberg *Mark Berry*
Arthur Schopenhauer *Peter B. Lewis*
Dmitry Shostakovich *Pauline Fairclough*
Adam Smith *Jonathan Conlin*
Susan Sontag *Jerome Boyd Maunsell*
Gertrude Stein *Lucy Daniel*
Stendhal *Francesco Manzini*
Igor Stravinsky *Jonathan Cross*
Rabindranath Tagore *Bashabi Fraser*
Pyotr Tchaikovsky *Philip Ross Bullock*
Dylan Thomas *John Goodby and Chris Wigginton*
Leo Tolstoy *Andrei Zorin*
Leon Trotsky *Paul Le Blanc*
Mark Twain *Kevin J. Hayes*
Richard Wagner *Raymond Furness*
Alfred Russel Wallace *Patrick Armstrong*
Simone Weil *Palle Yourgrau*
Tennessee Williams *Paul Ibell*
Ludwig Wittgenstein *Edward Kanterian*
Virginia Woolf *Ira Nadel*
Frank Lloyd Wright *Robert McCarter*

Maurice Ravel

Emily Kilpatrick

REAKTION BOOKS

In affectionate memory of Claude Moreau (1930–2024)

Published by Reaktion Books Ltd
2–4 Sebastian Street
London EC1V 0HE, UK

www.reaktionbooks.co.uk

First published 2025
Copyright © Emily Kilpatrick 2025

All rights reserved

EU GPSR Authorised Representative
Logos Europe, 9 rue Nicolas Poussin, 17000, La Rochelle, France
email: contact@logoseurope.eu

No part of this publication may be reproduced, stored in a retrieval system, or transmitted, in any form or by any means, electronic, mechanical, photocopying, recording or otherwise, without the prior permission of the publishers. No part of this publication may be used or reproduced in any manner for the purpose of training artificial intelligence technologies or systems.

Printed and bound in Great Britain by Bell & Bain, Glasgow

A catalogue record for this book is available from the British Library

ISBN 978 1 83639 089 3

Contents

Preface 7
1 The Engineer, the Basque and the Dandy 19
2 *Agent provocateur* 41
3 Dances with History 67
4 An Unknown Destination 93
5 The Compositional Machine 118
6 Dissolving 144

References 171
Bibliography 186
Acknowledgements 189
Photo Acknowledgements 191

Maurice Ravel, 1925.

Preface

> I am Basque; the Basques feel intensely but rarely show it, and then only to a very few.
> Maurice Ravel, to Jacques de Zogheb[1]

In December 1913 the critic Michel-Dmitri Calvocoressi began a survey of Maurice Ravel's life and work with a prophetic sentence. 'Of all the members of the younger French school,' he wrote, 'none – including even M. Claude Debussy – has irritated and perplexed critics more, nor been made the subject of warmer and more protracted discussion, than M. Maurice Ravel.'[2] More than a century later, if Ravel is still the focus of proliferating debate, reflection and scholarship, he remains remarkably elusive. The glossy surfaces of his music often seem to confound analysis, while his elliptical reflections may appear designed to deflect the critic (or the hapless biographer). Few composers, moreover, have so explicitly drawn the boundaries between self and creation, between private life and public art. Ravel insisted repeatedly that his work be considered on its own terms, its integrity unmarred by subjective or personal considerations, political events or ideological agenda. In interviews and articles, he emphasized the language not of artistry but of artisanship (*métier*); not of picturesque inspiration, but of discipline and rigorous discrimination.

And yet, and perhaps inevitably, few composers have so regularly been conflated with their output as has Maurice Ravel. This paradoxical fusion of the composer's life and work began early in his career, amid the hotbed of Parisian musical politics and polemic. Calvocoressi's article (written for a British audience) is a case in point. Calling attention to two of the charges that had been laid against Ravel's music over the previous decade, he notes that many writers have 'objected strongly to [its] "dryness" and "artificiality"' – then reflects, 'One might say that artificiality is natural to Maurice Ravel.' Emerging through musical criticism, the narratives of 'artifice' and 'imposture' were thus crystallized in the writings of Ravel's friends and apologists, then read back on to the composer himself: twenty years later, Calvocoressi would quote Ravel impatiently asking, 'Doesn't it ever occur to these people that I might be "artificial" by nature?'[3] Four years after Ravel's death, another of Calvocoressi's articles opened by skewering some of the tropes that he himself had helped to embed. 'Almost every one of those who have tried their hand at turning out portraits of [Ravel] as man and artist start on the assumption that there was something unusual and mysterious in his mental makeup', he wrote, 'and strive hard to define this mysterious something and to show it reflected in his music.'[4]

The determination to draw together that which the composer took pains to separate has not slackened: a recent collection of musicological essays, for example, bears the title *Unmasking Ravel*. This impulse stems, in part, from the composer's public persona, ironic, prickly, elegant and cryptic. It stems from his sustained explorations of creative practice and principle, which he articulated with an incisive clarity that few composers have matched (among many examples, perhaps the sharpest is his assertion that the sole test of good musical form was 'continuity of interest'[5]). And it stems, of course, from Ravel's music itself, and the seemingly irreconcilable contradictions between this deeply reserved, solitary man and his intensely colourful output, infused with the fantastic, bursting with the rhythms of the dance, and arching through the most unrestrainedly sensuous climaxes. It stems from his virtuosic orchestration, his diligent straining for the outermost limits of instrumental possibilities, and his delight in 'duping' the listener with unexpected timbral combinations. It stems from his distinctive harmonic language, in which a taste for piquant minor seconds and sevenths is fused with unabashedly lyrical melodic gestures, such as his signature swoon of a falling fourth. And it stems from his tendency to bind Romantic subjects within the clear lines of Classical forms, reconfigured from the inside out – a seeming conservatism that has long confined him in some quarters to the status of a *petit maître*.[6] For Ravel, 'originality' lay in teasing apart the strands of established practice, and reweaving them into something new. 'I don't myself see the need to break a window,' he said: 'I know how to open it.'[7]

Ravel grew to maturity in a society poised between the lures of past and future. Born in the aftermath of the *Année terrible* of

Fantasy and restraint: Ravel (with dragonflies) at the Viennese premiere of *L'Enfant et les sortilèges*, 1929.

1870–71, he spent his earliest years in a city appallingly scarred by siege and civil war, but alive with rebuilding and restoration. He was fourteen when, in 1889, Paris marked the centenary of the French Revolution with the Exposition Universelle – a festival whose crowning glory was the Tower designed by his father's one-time colleague Gustave Eiffel, and conceived as a monument to scientific progress and technical daring.

The France of Ravel's youth was concerned to the point of fixation with narratives of history and national identity. It is no coincidence that for his first published songs, *Deux épigrammes de Clément Marot* (1900), Ravel selected a Renaissance poet and evoked the textures of the harpsichord. His first opera, *L'Heure espagnole* (1911), is partly a commentary on forty years of French operatic obsessions, from *Tristan und Isolde* to *Pelléas et Mélisande* via Bizet's *Carmen*; his second, *L'Enfant et les sortilèges* (1925), openly parades its dialogues with the musical past and present. His early combative engagement with musical traditions (and institutions) later found more nuanced expression in his reckonings with his compositional predecessors and peers, in the press as well as on the musical page.

Ravel's concern with the lineaments of history and identity is equally apparent in his lifelong immersion in literature. Although he once deemed French a language 'not designed for poetry', in a 1922 article on Fauré's *mélodies* Ravel evoked its 'fleeting music [. . .] which is less obvious than that of Italian, for example, but how much more delicate and thus more precious!'[8] His own writing betrays his attentiveness to that 'fleeting music', his enjoyment of almost tactile patterns of rhythm and assonance evident in his predilection for unexpected verbs ('je turbine', he would write when hard at work), for slang, for galloping rhythms and unexpected comic twists. At other times his writing is shot through with real lyricism: one letter of February 1906 evokes 'belles journées de gelée, qui font les forêts si féeriques!' ('beautiful frozen days, rendering the forests magical!'), its luscious alliteration couched in near-impeccable dactylic feet.[9]

'Almost all [Ravel's] *œuvre*', wrote the critic René Chalupt in 1925, 'unfolds upon a literary background that, indirectly or directly, prompts the patterns of his inspiration.'[10] Ravel nourished a Baudelairean fascination with refracting one art through the prism of another, from his pianistic translations of Aloysius Bertrand's prose-poetry (*Gaspard de la Nuit*) and the fairytales of the age of Louis xv (*Ma mère l'Oye*), to his early overture *Shéhérazade*, a never-realized concerto on Alain-Fournier's *Le Grand Meaulnes*, and the putative scherzo of his Piano Trio, which adopts the title and patterning of the poetic 'Pantoum'. He claimed that his *Trois poèmes de Stéphane Mallarmé* 'transposed' not just the words but 'the literary procedures' of his poet, and explained to the writer Jules Renard of *Histoires naturelles* that he had intended 'to express in music what you have expressed in words'.[11]

In tracing Ravel's life as both man and musician, then, this biography holds to these guiding threads of language, literature and historical conversation, for it is here that we find the most revealing intersections of practice and aesthetic – and perhaps, too, the most sustainable accommodations of self and art. The six chapters follow Ravel through his early years, his Conservatoire training and his first musical ventures; his emergence on the Parisian compositional scene early in the new century; the firm establishment of his career from about 1907; his experiences during and immediately after the First World War; his role in the changing compositional landscape of the 1920s; and his last years, from the successful American tour in 1928 through his progressive and tragic incapacitation in the 1930s.

We begin, though, with a brief sketch of Ravel himself. A small, spare man, and conscious of his diminutive stature, even his most casual photographs and portraits embody a concentrated energy. He had a fine-drawn, angular face, with piercing brown eyes and heavy brows that remained dark even when his hair turned silver. Meticulous and unfailingly elegant, Ravel, as his friend Léon-Paul Fargue wrote, 'would never appear scruffy or unkempt, even to his intimates'.[12] His American hosts in 1928 were startled to discover that he had brought 20 pairs of pyjamas and 57 ties; five years later one young associate wrote, 'One does not usually notice a man's clothes, but I am always intrigued by speculations as to what he would be wearing next.'[13]

Although he maintained a careful distance from political theatres, Ravel was unquestionably a man of the left, a *dreyfusard* who took the socialist newspaper *Le Populaire* and counted Léon Blum among his friends. When he engaged in the machinations of musical politics, it was consistently in the interests of a progressive internationalism, a stance he made most public when he spoke out against the Ligue nationale pour la défense de la musique française in 1917. He was not religious, referring to himself at least once as an atheist.[14] His parents had likewise been untroubled by convention in matters of conscience and religion: his mother regarded matters of faith with the practical tempering of a poor and marginalized childhood, his father with the intellectual coolness of the engineer, a determined rationality that he plainly transmitted to his elder son.

Ravel had a dry, biting wit and a lively sense of the ridiculous. Although he sought to cultivate an ironic distance, when anger flared it was often rapid and acute. He was frequently abrupt and sometimes unreasonable, his bluntness startling those who expected polite formulations. He permitted no liberties of performers and fought tooth and nail – including in the press, and through his lawyers – to defend the integrity of his work. Compromise did not come easily, and he had little tolerance for anyone whom he considered to have fallen short of his own rigid standards: 'He could not abide the slightest untruth,' the composer and conductor Manuel Rosenthal reflected. He broke off a long friendship with the statesman Paul Painlevé when he found that Painlevé had falsely denied being a Freemason, explaining, 'I couldn't care less whether he is a mason or not; it's that he lied to me.'[15]

In a 1938 obituary Calvocoressi wrote, 'When expressing his views on art or any other matter, [Ravel] was always definite and firm, and often trenchant. He had the utmost confidence in his judgements – a confidence rooted in [a] clear knowledge of himself.'[16] He was a punishing and sometimes infuriating collaborator, but a generous one; a demanding friend, but intensely loyal; an exacting teacher, who laid down boundaries to watch his students discover how to breach them. He liked to have his own way, his younger brother noted, but he wanted others to agree with him in considering it the *best* way – 'otherwise his pleasure was spoiled'.[17]

Ravel's friends loved him dearly, and their memoirs are flooded not just with respect and admiration but with profound tenderness and humour – although his vagaries could provoke amused bewilderment or unalloyed exasperation, too. Calvocoressi wrote of the 'aloofness' that masked a 'warm-heartedness and fundamental ingenuousness'; Ravel's pupil and amanuensis Roland-Manuel stressed that although his courteous reserve was slow to dissolve, 'Ravel was the surest, the most faithful and most profoundly affectionate of friends.'[18]

Ravel maintained few casual friendships, preferring instead the company of a small circle of close friends. 'He was no *boulevardier*,' wrote Fargue, for his uncompromising honesty rendered him as ill suited to the casual jousting of the Montmartre cafés as to the more rarefied conversation of the salons.[19] It was not uncommon for him to disappear midway through a formal dinner, to be found telling stories or playing games with the children in the nursery. Such vanishing acts were perhaps a marker not just of Ravel's oft-noted ease with children but of a limited capacity for charged social situations, and the self-knowledge to recognize when to beat a retreat. 'Living cannot be easy for him,' wrote one *New York Times* journalist in 1928.[20]

Many sketches of Ravel describe a childlike (or 'childish') innocence, manifested particularly in his delight in new clothes and trinkets. In other accounts, his stubborn insistence on certain odd things – belongings, habits, opinions – is sometimes cast as the behaviour of a 'spoilt child', a carryover from a peculiarly intense relationship with his mother. Ravel's mind could indeed stumble over small, seemingly unimportant details: Rosenthal told of him agonizing for 45 minutes over the ideal form of address with which to begin a simple letter of introduction, for example.[21] He was often unable to think his way past unexpected alterations or impediments, a trait that only hardened at moments of stress. One concert in 1930 was seriously delayed by the last-minute disappearance of the handkerchief for the pocket of his suit jacket;

On the balcony of Le Belvédère, 1930.

although the pianist Robert Casadesus offered his handkerchief as a substitute, Ravel refused because the initials were not his own.[22] That disproportionate response hints at something more fundamental than 'dandyism' or the 'spoilt child'. It was not that Ravel *wouldn't* walk on stage, but that he *couldn't*.

More serious disruptions had more profound impact. The periods of Ravel's greatest confusion and misery were those when the rhythms of his daily life were shattered: the first months of the First World War; the years that followed his mother's death in 1917. If it is hardly surprising that such times of intense national and personal trauma were most difficult to navigate, noteworthy in Ravel's responses to both situations is a deep sense of deracination, caused by the upending of the securities on which he relied: home, family, and the rounds and rhythms of his professional life.

All these traits – a need for order, routine and control; occasionally rigid thinking, and a certain lack of awareness or capacity regarding social norms; 'masking' and the careful cultivation of a public self – suggest that in seeking a more holistic approach to Ravel and his music, we might usefully draw on a twenty-first-century understanding of neurodivergence. Ravel's public persona – sometimes provocative, sometimes pretentious, always elusive – was surely constructed of necessity by a man for whom acting in the world was possible only through certain accommodations. 'I'm not very cheerful [. . .] when I'm alone, *because* when there's a crowd no one surpasses me [in cheerfulness],' he wrote to a friend in 1919.[23] Those permitted within his boundaries told story upon story of his warmth, spontaneity and unquenchable humour. Rosenthal would recall with some emotion a conversation with the composer in his last years, when, as they were laughing together over a silly anecdote,

> I forgot my usual address, and suddenly said to him 'No, Ravel, but don't you think . . .' And then I pulled myself up immediately: it was the first time that I had said 'Ravel' and not 'maître'! And he looked at me with that eye of his, gentle and teasing as a squirrel. And he said to me: 'Finally!'[24]

Ravel, Fargue wrote simply, was 'a profoundly sensitive and good man'.[25]

One facet of Ravel's life has, by its very absence, prompted much speculation and contention. The first of his known letters, sent in July 1895 to an unidentified female correspondent, concludes suggestively, 'I place at your feet, in the conventional manner, my most respectful greetings (though inside I'm really thinking in another sense . . .).'[26] But the 2,500 items of documented correspondence that follow offer no trace of a sexual relationship. Although few composers have played so powerfully on tropes of love, sex and raw emotion, all his life Ravel remained determinedly single. Several friends testified to his frank confession that the demands of his craft were all-consuming, making an intimate relationship untenable. (It is worth noting, too, that from his late twenties until his early forties, Ravel bore significant responsibility for the care of his elderly and progressively incapacitated parents.) His intense need for solitude, his lurching between extreme lassitude and frantic activity, would, he knew, have made him an impossible partner.

Several anecdotal accounts suggest that Ravel had occasional dealings with (female) prostitutes, and that in later life he maintained a discreet 'arrangement' with a married woman near his home in Montfort-l'Amaury; the latter relationship quietly passed into local lore and was cited by several elderly residents in conversation with the author in the early 2000s. There is no evidence that he was homosexual, beyond the circumstantial factors of close male friends, some of whom were gay; a penchant for dandyism; the absence of substantiated heterosexual relationships; and one song, 'L'Indifférent' (*Shéhérazade*), on a text by his friend Tristan Klingsor (Léon Leclère), that carries an unquestionably homoerotic charge. If Ravel was indeed gay, it is peculiar in the extreme that no trace of any relationship filtered into the mountain of primary source material that surrounds his life and work, notwithstanding the protectiveness of the many friends invested in the shaping of his legacy.[27] (By way of comparison, the long-term homosexual relationships separately maintained by two of Ravel's

Notes for Ravel's 'Autobiographical Sketch', 1928. This fascinating and vital summary of Ravel's life and work was dictated to Roland-Manuel; originally intended for the Aeolian Company, it remained unpublished until 1938.

slightly older colleagues, Pierre de Bréville and Charles Bordes, are clearly traceable in the correspondence of both composers and their circles.)

Moreover, reading 'L'Indifférent', a restrainedly lascivious evocation of a beautiful boy, as bearing directly on the composer's own sexuality is doubly risky. Entailing a conflation of life and work in precisely the manner Ravel rejected, it also minimizes the compositional mastery required to balance the cool distance of the observer with the erotic charge of the subject, and the hair's-breadth precision of making art at the limits of social acceptability. (Writing of a planned British concert in 1907, Ravel admitted jokingly that the song 'might frighten the Londoners'.[28]) We might note, too, that the implicit homoeroticism there pales beside the lavishly heteronormative and far more explicit 'Nahandove' (*Chansons madécasses*), never mind the orgasmic cats of *L'Enfant et les sortilèges*.

Crucially, if Ravel did indeed channel through his art the passions that found no expression in life, we should be wary of the reciprocal assertion that such a denial caused him particular pain or stress. Those who knew the composer best emphasized above all his uncompromising integrity. For all his intense *pudeur*, his outward masks and his extravagant dressing gowns, he was a man who, one senses, would have found the concealment of a fundamental truth both emotionally and intellectually unsustainable.

For more than a century, Ravel's life and work have been framed as a series of contradictions and elaborate disguises: therein lies both the scholarly puzzle and the artistic lure. If this biography plays among these dissonances and disjunctions – as indeed did Ravel himself, on many occasions – it nevertheless seeks to trace a life of utterly consistent purpose and expression. It offers a portrait of one of the most fascinating minds of his age, and of a music that remains at the heart of the performing repertoire, beguiling, moving, challenging and intriguing audiences now as it did in the composer's lifetime.

1
The Engineer, the Basque and the Dandy

At seven o'clock one chilly morning in January 1869, an extraordinary vehicle appeared on the peaceful suburban streets of Neuilly-sur-Seine. It was a three-wheeled automobile, propelled by steam generated by an internal combustion engine. The civic authorities had granted the vehicle's inventor, a Swiss-born engineer named Pierre-Joseph Ravel, permission to test his vehicle on a prescribed stretch of road, accompanied by two policemen on foot. So cold was the morning, and so unenthusiastic the escort, that it took only a little encouragement for the policemen to retreat to a nearby café and regale themselves with hot grog. Thus unobserved by authority, Pierre-Joseph proceeded to drive his vehicle at a majestic 6 kilometres per hour (3¾ mph) all the way to Saint-Denis, returning two hours later. He could not be charged for violating the terms of his permit, since his escort had to admit that they had been drinking on duty.[1] Meticulous design and technical daring, a persuasively smooth manner, and the occasionally outrageous disregard of regulations: in this story proudly recounted by Maurice Ravel's father we may easily trace something of his legacy to his elder son.

Pierre-Joseph's vehicle was not long-lived: his workshop was destroyed amid the chaos of the Siege of Paris (1870–71). Rather than trying immediately to rebuild his business in the devastated city, he returned to Spain, where he had worked as a railway engineer in the late 1850s and early 1860s. It was in Madrid, or the nearby gardens of Aranjuez (as his son was romantically to insist), in 1872 that the forty-year-old Pierre-Joseph Ravel encountered

Marie Delouart, Madrid, c. 1870.

Marie Delouart. Marie had travelled to Spain from her native Basque country as assistant and model to a Paris *modiste*. Like Pierre-Joseph, she came from a border region: she was born in the fishing village of Ciboure, abutting the town of Saint-Jean-de-Luz. But while Pierre-Joseph's family could be traced back through several centuries of respectable Genevois smallholders and craftsmen, Marie's origins were among the very poor. She was one of a distinct local population known as *kaskarotes*, a people of Spanish and Roma descent, historically persecuted and marginalized (they were long thought to harbour leprosy). Marie was illegitimate, as was her mother, Sabine, who sold fish on the quays of Ciboure; her childhood and much of her ancestry remain a blank. She spoke good Spanish but faulty French, and she was barely literate (her one surviving letter, sent to her elder son in 1916, is strewn with grammatical and spelling errors). But she was resourceful and strong-minded: her trajectory from illegitimacy and poverty to the fashion boutiques of Madrid is remarkable in itself.

However unlikely their meeting, after a brief courtship Pierre-Joseph Ravel and Marie Delouart were married, in Paris, on 3 April 1873. Towards the end of 1874 Marie, by now five or six months pregnant, travelled back to Ciboure to care for her mother in her final illness. After Sabine's death, Marie chose not to make the arduous journey back to the capital, remaining instead in the care of her relatives. Her first son, Joseph-Maurice Ravel, was thus born in the Basque country of his maternal ancestors, at ten o'clock in the evening on 7 March 1875.

In June, Marie and her baby returned to Paris, accompanied by her aunt Gracieuse Billac (known to the family as Gachoucha). They joined Pierre-Joseph at 40 rue des Martyrs in the ninth arrondissement, midway between the newly inaugurated Opéra Garnier and the summit of Montmartre – where, within days of their arrival, the first stones of the Basilique du Sacré-Cœur were laid. The basilica rising slowly on the hilltop would have been continually at the edge of Maurice Ravel's vision throughout his childhood and youth: although the family moved to other apartments in 1880 (29 rue Victor-Massé) and 1886 (73 rue Pigalle), they remained in the same district, around the foot of Montmartre.

The 1880 move was perhaps necessitated by the birth, on 13 June 1878, of a second son, Édouard John. He was named after his paternal uncle, a painter of quiet distinction, whose semi-regular visits to the capital over the next decade produced a series of family portraits: Pierre-Joseph, in 1880; two small sailor-suited nephews, most likely in 1882; and, three years later, a striking pastel of his sister-in-law. Both Pierre-Joseph's sons remained close to their uncle as they grew to adulthood, and when the elder Édouard died in 1920 he made Maurice his heir. The legacy enabled Ravel's purchase of Le Belvédère in Montfort-l'Amaury, where the paired miniatures of

1882 still hang by his writing desk, and the portrait of Marie above the piano.

Aged 42 and 35 in the spring of 1875, Pierre-Joseph and Marie Ravel were older than average new parents. Nevertheless, they seem to have settled contentedly into their roles. Marie adored and was fiercely protective of her children, and the family circle was close and warm: decades later an elderly friend would write to Ravel of 'your good parents [. . .] who were always so loving to you and Édouard, and whose joys were all concentrated in their children'.[2] Pierre-Joseph, by now energetically re-establishing his business in Paris, took his sons with him to factories, workshops and exhibitions. 'It was these machines,' Ravel recalled, 'their clicking and roaring, which, with the Spanish folksongs sung to me nightly as a berceuse by my mother, formed my first instruction in music!'[3] A family photograph taken around 1884 shows Édouard sprawling on his father's knee with the look of a child who has had enough of posing. Maurice leans on Pierre-Joseph's other side, an arm draped around his shoulders. The physical ease and tenderness of the image

Pierre-Joseph Ravel with Édouard and Maurice, c. 1884.

suggest a man comfortable in his fatherhood, and children secure in their parents' affection.

Pierre-Joseph passed to his sons a focused and brilliant intellect, a tradition of artisanship and a sympathy for the arts (he had himself studied the piano at the Geneva Conservatoire). But although Ravel remained close to his Swiss relatives, and visited the region relatively frequently in adulthood, never did he claim a Swiss-French or Savoyard identity. Deeply as he loved his father, it was Marie who was to form the emotional anchor of his life, and his maternal heritage to which he felt most closely allied. 'I am Basque,' he would declare proudly, eager to assert an inheritance not just of descent but of birth.[4] Even though he had left Ciboure as an infant, as an adult he wrote of the region as his 'homeland', maintained close relationships with Basque friends and family, and spent long summers there whenever he could.

The embrace of a provincial ancestry was not atypical for a Parisian of Ravel's generation. Industrialization and urbanization had spawned a compensatory nostalgia for the landscapes of childhood and family, and the mythologized rural *terroir*. It is clear, however, that Ravel felt truly at home in the Basque country. As a child he must have heard at least some Basque spoken, since it was the first language of both Marie and Gachoucha (who stayed with them for extended periods of Ravel's childhood). As an adult he took pride in speaking a little of the language himself, his composer's ear delighting in its extreme difference and difficulty. He happily sprinkled letters to acquaintances in Saint-Jean-de-Luz with Basque words and phrases, and could read letters he received from a Conservatoire classmate in 'the most elegant Basque'. 'Never forget a Basque has two homelands,' he wrote to a colleague in 1920.[5] Embracing his Basque identity was also one way by which Ravel maintained a sense of his 'otherness': it allowed him, when he chose, to remain an outsider.

Of Ravel's schooling almost nothing is known, although he must have attended a local elementary school. One class photograph survives, from about 1885, in which the Ravel brothers are easily distinguished by their matching sailor suits and collar-length

School group, Paris, 1885. Ravel is in the middle row, second from left, with Édouard beside him.

hair. All Ravel himself said of his early education was that – to his father's delight – he liked and was good at mathematics.[6] His formal musical tuition began at the hands of Henry Ghys, a friend of Emmanuel Chabrier, in 1882. After Ravel's first piano lesson on 31 May, Ghys recorded in his diary that his seven-year-old pupil 'appears intelligent', although he added resignedly, 'I now appear to be destined for teaching children.'[7] Ravel soon adopted a pragmatic approach to his practice, later confessing that he 'would only work like a taxi: in order to produce the slightest effort, I had to be paid.'[8] (The going rate was 10 sous per half-hour.)

In 1887 Ravel's piano lessons were augmented by study in harmony and counterpoint, and in 1888 he began to prepare for the Conservatoire, taking private lessons with one of the professors, Émile Descombes (a former associate of Chopin), and attending a series of evening piano classes where the teachers included another professor, Charles de Bériot. At those classes Marie Ravel was delighted to encounter several Spanish speakers: not just Bériot himself (son of the great soprano Maria Malibran) but his assistant Santiago Riera, who was to become a long-standing friend and mentor to Ravel; and, perhaps most importantly, a thirteen-year-old Catalan pianist named Ricardo Viñes, and his mother, Dolores. The mothers quickly became friends: 'This evening we went, for the first time, to visit the long-haired boy whose name is Mauricio,' Viñes recorded in his diary on 23 November 1888. Ravel's hair fascinated Viñes for some time: on 7 December he writes, 'in the evening, to Mme Ravel's (Mama of the long-haired boy)', and two weeks later, 'with Mama visiting the *chevelu* [hairy boy], that is, Mauricio Ravel'.[9]

On 4 November 1889 Viñes and Ravel auditioned together for the Conservatoire. Ravel was accepted into Eugène Anthiome's preparatory class, but Viñes, who had been auditing classes and studying privately with Bériot since his arrival in Paris two years earlier, vaulted directly into the senior class. At their first examinations in January 1890, Bériot reported that Viñes, who performed Chopin's *Barcarolle*, had 'astonished everyone with the rapidity of his progress'. Ravel too played Chopin – one of the Polonaises – but his teacher's reports were much more temperate: 'some skill', Anthiome noted, and 'fairly conscientious work'. In the end-of-year examination of 1890 Ravel is described as 'assez doué' ('fairly gifted'), and in the January and July examinations of 1891 he is simply a 'bon élève' ('good student'); Viñes, meanwhile, had 'outclassed all his peers'. Nevertheless, in the final examinations of 1891 Ravel won the *premier prix* that allowed him to join his friend in Bériot's class, and to enter the harmony class of Émile Pessard.[10]

In neither of his new classes did Ravel shine. Pessard initially described him as 'bien doué', but later reports moderate this assessment to 'assez doué' and note a tendency to absent-mindedness; by January 1895 he had been relegated to 'pas mal doué' ('not ungifted'). Bériot's assessments likewise suggest cautious enthusiasm, tempered increasingly by the frustration of a teacher who knows his student is capable of far more than he is giving: 'works inconsistently', he reported in June 1894. His reports praise an expressive, passionate pianism, which sometimes came at the cost of strict accuracy: 'A tendency to reach for big effects. Needs to be reined in,' he noted of Ravel's attempt at Schumann's op. 17 *Fantaisie* in January 1894.[11]

Although Viñes had long outstripped Ravel as a pianist, the boys remained close friends. They went to concerts and plays together, and Viñes's diary records many afternoons spent sight-reading duets and 'trying out new chords'. But they also played board games and built models, stargazed, drew (Ravel had an excellent eye), read, and explored the city and its surroundings. 'We took the boat to Saint-Cloud and walked through the Garches woods to Ville-d'Avray [. . .] on the way back, near Marnes, Maurice found 10 centimes in the woods. We had a lot of fun,' Viñes wrote happily in August 1892.[12]

While Ravel had attempted some scholastic composition exercises in his early teens, his first independent compositions date from 1893, a year marked by certain crucial musical encounters.

Pencil sketch by Ravel, late 1880s.

That summer he made the acquaintance of another habitué of the ninth arrondissement, Erik Satie, then the resident pianist at the Auberge du Clou and a regular at the Café de la Nouvelle Athènes on the place Pigalle (just yards from the Ravel apartment on rue Pigalle). While accounts of their introduction differ, it was probably at the Nouvelle Athènes – which was, after all, his local – that Pierre-Joseph introduced his sons not just to Satie but to Debussy, who had many friends and acquaintances in this corner of the city and had been for several years a friend of Satie's.

Soon after this first encounter, Ravel would reportedly 'stupefy' Pessard by bringing Satie's *Gymnopédies* to his harmony class.[13] He also produced his earliest surviving song, *Ballade de la Reine morte d'aimer*, whose luminous modal textures, as he would admit in the 'Autobiographical Sketch' of 1928, clearly betray Satie's influence. But the piano piece he presented to Pessard that autumn, *Sérénade [grotesque]*, looks not to Satie but to Chabrier – 'the one composer who has influenced me above all others', as he wrote in 1929.[14] While that influence betrays itself most transparently in his early works, Ravel's whole output was to bear the imprint of Chabrier's prophetic harmonic genius, the clarity and wit of his musical rhetoric, and the uncontainable flair of his orchestration.

Ravel met Chabrier just once, on 8 February 1893. He and Viñes were preparing the older composer's two-piano *Valses romantiques* for a concert and visited him in his apartment on the nearby avenue Trudaine for a coaching session. 'He spent an hour and a half with us, and told us that we played very well, and with good taste,' Viñes recorded.[15] Decades later, Jean Françaix gave a marvellous (if otherwise uncorroborated) account of Chabrier's response: 'two very well-dressed young people came and played my *Trois valses romantiques*. The first played very well; the second played like a pig, but what a musician!'[16]

The biting sonorities and exuberant textures of Ravel's *Sérénade grotesque* nod most directly to Chabrier's recently published *Bourrée fantasque* (the adjective *grotesque*, which is first recorded only in the 'Autobiographical Sketch', perhaps underlines that debt through its neatly parallel assonances). Transparently experimental, the piece feels more like a series of colourful ideas than a unified whole, its syncopations uncontrolled and its structure flabby; Ravel appears never to have contemplated publishing it. Nevertheless, the character and energy of the piano writing are obvious, as is Ravel's natural fluency in 'Spanish' mode: certain melodic and harmonic turns clearly foreshadow 'Alborada del gracioso', from the *Miroirs* he would realize a dozen years later. Ravel's classmate Gustave Mouchet recalled that Pessard tried but failed to make sense of the *Sérénade* at the piano, eventually giving up and asking Ravel to play it himself. 'Ah yes, you've produced a very curious effect here,' Pessard concluded, 'but you seem to be riding fantasies; you must control your thoughts, take fewer liberties. Well – who knows, perhaps you will create a new style for us.'[17]

At the Conservatoire examinations in July 1895, Ravel failed to achieve a prize for either piano or harmony. It was his third consecutive failure and so, in accordance with regulations, he was ejected from both classes, five and a half years of study brought to an abrupt and inglorious conclusion. Nevertheless, there seems to have been no suggestion from his family that he should abandon his chosen profession. He gave occasional piano lessons and earned some intermittent wages as an accompanist; he also took on jobbing compositional work, arranging a group of Corsican songs for a lecture-demonstration early in 1896, and producing some unadventurous dance music for a salon ballet, *La Parade*, in 1898. A thoughtful journal entry penned by Viñes in November 1896, however, suggests that Ravel's early twenties were shadowed by precarity and disappointment. The two young men had gone to the Concerts Lamoureux to hear a programme including the Prelude to Wagner's *Tristan und Isolde*:

> Just as I was thinking to myself that there could be nothing in creation as sublime and as divine as that superb Prelude, at that moment Ravel touched me on the hand and said, 'It's always like this, every time that I hear it.' And indeed, Ravel, who can appear so cool and cynical, Ravel the super-eccentric 'decadent', Ravel was trembling convulsively and weeping like a child.

In his emotional reticence, his opinions and his literary tastes, Viñes continued, Ravel might appear affected, deliberately recherché – and yet,

> I see that this chap was born with those inclinations, those tastes and those opinions, and when he expresses them, he doesn't do it to appear snobbish or to follow the fashion, but because he really feels it [. . .] In the eyes of the vulgar [Ravel] appears a failure, but in reality he is a superior mind and artist.[18]

Barricading himself against the whispers of failure, at 21 Ravel was cultivating a persona of cool, dandified eccentricity: a few months later he would pass Viñes his copies of Jules Barbey d'Aurevilly's essays on Beau Brummel, and on dandyism. The fashioning and control of his image in these early years was in part a declaration of intent, a deliberate drawing of his distance from a professional world that had so far refused to open to him.

However he chose to present himself, and despite the uncertainty of his métier, by November 1895 Ravel had produced several 'new, strange compositions' (as Viñes recorded), probably including *Menuet antique*, the song *Un grand sommeil noir* and the two-piano 'Habanera'.[19] The last of these represents a far more fluent venture into 'Spanishness': if *Sérénade grotesque* has a slight air of trying to do everything all at once, the 'Habanera' has the assurance of a piece that does one thing extremely well indeed. The first of Ravel's works to feel utterly cogent and distinctively his own, the composer would recycle it almost unamended a dozen years later, as the third movement of his *Rapsodie espagnole*. Its characteristic sonority of a dominant seventh chord above a dissonant pedal would become a signature gesture, infusing such later works as 'Alborada del gracioso', *Vocalise-Étude en forme de habanera* and *L'Heure espagnole*.

More obviously indebted to Chabrier is *Menuet antique*, whose middle section responds to the equivalent 'trio' of Chabrier's 'Menuet pompeux' (from the *Pièces pittoresques* of 1880). There are echoes, too, of a more genuinely 'antique' heritage: the opening semiquaver motions, passing from hand to hand through gently sequential suspensions, are faintly reminiscent of some of François Couperin's *allemande* movements ('La Logivière' (5e Ordre), for example, which shares Ravel's three-sharp key signature and unusual 'Majestueusement' tempo heading). As a Conservatoire pupil Ravel is likely to have known the collection *Les Clavecinistes français* (1887), edited by piano professor Louis Diémer, who championed this repertoire throughout the 1890s. Perhaps, too, he recognized the echoes of the *clavecinistes* in Chabrier's *Pièces pittoresques* themselves: César Franck, on first hearing some of those pieces in 1881, reportedly exclaimed, 'We have just heard something extraordinary. This music links our era to that of Couperin and Rameau.'[20] *Menuet antique* is an early example of Ravel's capacity to refract one inspiration through the frame of another, and of his concern with not just historical 'objects' but the through-lines of inheritance.

These interactions with both recent and more distant musical pasts found a parallel in Ravel's literary explorations, in which his companion and chronicler was again Ricardo Viñes. From afternoons spent trawling the riverside *bouquinistes* to their studies of Baudelaire and Poe, Viñes's diary testifies to an attentiveness to unusual works and rare editions, and an active engagement with literary currents. In November 1891 Viñes lent Ravel Poe's *Histoires extraordinaires* (in Baudelaire's translation); nine months later he recorded, 'Maurice showed me a very gloomy picture he'd done after Poe's *Descent into the Maelström*. Today, as I watched, he did another one, also very dark, after Poe's *Manuscript Found in a Bottle*.' In 1893 the two eighteen-year-olds were swapping Baudelaire sonnets; the following September Ravel picked up 'some [hitherto] unpublished writings' of Poe's at a bookstall; and a few weeks after that, Viñes went to the Ravels' apartment to return some Baudelaire he'd borrowed,

> and there I saw the six censored and forbidden extracts of *Les Fleurs du mal*; needless to say, they're the most beautiful. When Ravel has written them out, from a copy that a friend has passed to him, he will lend them to me so that I can copy them myself.[21]

By 1896 they were deep in Huysmans, Rimbaud, Henri de Régnier, Mallarmé, and Maeterlinck's *Serres chaudes*.

In that list we find many of the writers who were to furnish Ravel with not just song texts and epigraphs but a philosophy of craft. Perhaps most interesting in that context is Charles Baudelaire, whose words Ravel never set but whose influence was quietly decisive, his writings on poetry, art and the creative process resonating through Ravel's oeuvre. In 1931 Ravel would assert, 'I read in a thoroughly professional manner, as if I were a writer. The same holds true for painting: I cannot look at a painting as an amateur, but rather as a painter.'[22] Baudelaire offered not just a theory but a virtuosic enactment of such creative 'translation': 'the best critique of a painting might be a sonnet, or an elegy,' he wrote in 'Salon de 1846'.[23] Ravel in turn would liken Chabrier's 'Mélancolie' to Manet's *Olympia*, the spirit of the painting 'simply transposed to another medium'.[24]

It is thus unsurprising that the first years of Ravel's composing life produced more songs than anything else, although almost all of them remained long unpublished. *Ballade de la Reine morte d'aimer* was followed late in 1894 by an incomplete setting of Verlaine's 'Le ciel est, par-dessus le toit' (within weeks of Fauré's searing setting of the same poem, as *Prison*). In August 1895 Ravel returned to Verlaine with the bleakly chromatic *Un grand sommeil noir*, whose textures and vocal writing would be echoed three years later in the equally cheerless *Si morne!*, on a poem by the Belgian Symbolist Émile Verhaeren. Then, in the last weeks of 1896, Ravel set one text by Clément Marot, 'D'Anne jouant de l'espinette', and another by a writer of such determined modernism that no established composer had yet published a song on his poetry: Stéphane Mallarmé.

The violinist Hélène Jourdan-Morhange, who became one of Ravel's closest friends, observed wryly that his chosen poetic texts often seemed 'unsuited to being clothed with music'.[25] He would be drawn to writers who juggled openly with the ungainly rhythms and awkward vowels of the French language, and to texts that play with the expressive tension between meaning and assonance. Verlaine's 'Un grand sommeil noir' ('A great, dark sleep') is a poem of taut alliteration ('Je suis un berceau/ Qu'une main balance/ Au creux d'un caveau/ Silence, silence!' – 'I am a cradle/ Rocked by a hand/ In the depths of a vault/ Silence, silence!'), while Verhaeren's 'Si morne' ('So bleak') conjures desolation through aural monotony. 'Pourrir, immensément emailloté d'ennui/ Être l'ennui qui se replie de la nuit' ('To rot, intensely swathed in ennui/ To be that ennui that withdraws into the night'), reads the penultimate strophe, the paradoxical heaviness of the repeated light *i* vowels underscored in Ravel's song by their setting on a literal monotone. Marot's more playful verses sparkle with wordplay and alliteration, evident in the witty juggling of homonyms (*dieux*, *d'yeulx* (eyes), mélo*dieux*; *voy*, *voix*) in 'D'Anne jouant de l'espinette', and the pile-up of fricatives in 'D'Anne qui me jecta de la neige', which Ravel would set in 1899 ('Anne, par *j*eu, me *j*ecta de la nei*g*e' – 'Anne, in jest, threw snow at me').

    Mallarmé's 'Sainte' offers a more fundamental intersection of music and language, expression and form: the poet himself described it as 'a small melodic poem, made above all with music in mind'.[26] Deliberately 'foursquare' in its framing (four quatrains, couched in octosyllables), the poem unfolds as a single long sentence, in which the first two strophes each conjure a single image (the tarnished viol, the old book), but the third and fourth are bound together syntactically and expressively through their evocation of the vivifying angel. Poetic meaning is conveyed through the articulation of poetic structure, the old arts fused and reborn in a new creative expression.

    Like 'Soupir' and 'Placet futile', which Ravel was to set in 1913, 'Sainte' dates from a period in which Mallarmé's conscious quest for a 'musicalized' language had been galvanized by Poe (whose poetry he translated into French) and Baudelaire.[27] Ravel's setting, composed when he was just 21, thus represents the mingled legacies of three of the writers who marked him most deeply. If its ninth chords, non-functional progressions and modal colours again betray the influence of Satie, *Sainte* is nevertheless his first song of indisputable maturity, responding to Mallarmé's poetic imperative in its progressively more sinuous intertwining of voice and piano. Such was Ravel's confidence in *Sainte* that he allowed it to be published more than ten years later, in the spring of 1907 (while simultaneously dismissing *Un grand sommeil noir* and *Si morne!* as 'too juvenile [to be issued]').[28] As Viñes had incisively observed just a month before the composition of *Sainte,* behind the facade of the dandy was an artist of ever-clarifying métier and intent.

In compositional terms, these songs of the 1890s brought an increasingly sophisticated integration of form and gesture, a growing appreciation of the musicality inherent in poetic rhythm and assonance, and a heightened attention to the possibilities of vocal declamation. What Ravel lacked, as he well knew, was a command of orchestration and the rigour to sustain larger musical structures. In 1897, therefore, he began private lessons with André Gedalge, who was both an outstanding technician and a gifted teacher. Gedalge, Ravel later wrote, 'taught me how to realize the possibilities and the attempts at form that have been observed in my early works. His teaching had a singular clarity: with him, one understood immediately that craft is something more than scholastic abstraction.'[29] An early product of Ravel's lessons with Gedalge was the first movement of a violin sonata, composed in April 1897. Although Ravel never sought either to complete or to publish the work (which was issued only in 1975), Arbie Orenstein notes pre-echoes of the 1914 Piano Trio in the turn of its opening phrase and the Basque flavour of its irregular rhythms.[30]

At the end of 1897 it was perhaps Ravel's study of counterpoint and timbre that prompted another two-piano piece, 'Entre cloches', an exuberant and rhythmically sophisticated play of bell sonorities. It was with 'Entre cloches' and the 'Habanera', collectively titled *Sites auriculaires,* that Ravel made his début at the Société nationale de musique (SNM), on 5 March 1898. The performance, given by Viñes and Marthe Dron, was not a success: Viñes recorded that he and Dron found themselves a quaver out of alignment in 'Entre cloches', producing 'an unspeakable effect' as sonorities that were meant to be heard alternately fell cacophonously together.[31] Nor did the audience – or the critics – approve of Ravel's title. '*Sites auriculaires*?!?!' was all the prominent critic Hugues Imbert had to say of the work, while in *Le Progrès artistique* Paul Porthmann was equally lavish in his punctuation, if not his enthusiasm. '*Sites* (??) *auriculaires* (!!!!) offered a lighter note,' Porthmann wrote, describing the 'Habanera' as a 'piano-tuners' duo' and 'Entre cloches' as 'consumptive'.[32]

Despite this inauspicious début, the early months of 1898 had presented Ravel with a series of promising opportunities. In January he saw his music in print for the first time, as *Menuet antique* was issued by Chabrier's former publisher Enoch. At this stage of his career Ravel was doubtless delighted to be published by anyone, but it would have been particularly satisfying to see his music appear under the same imprint as both his idol and his teacher Gedalge (who must have recommended him to Enoch). Enoch, in turn, perhaps recognized that Ravel's *Menuet* might usefully draw attention to a group of four piano pieces by Chabrier, which he had just issued as a posthumous collection. Viñes recorded that Enoch had given him a pile of newly published scores, including the Chabrier pieces and Ravel's *Menuet*, and suggested that he programme them together in a forthcoming concert.[33]

It was also in January 1898 that Ravel returned to the Conservatoire as a pupil in Gabriel Fauré's composition class. Fauré was something of an anti-establishment figure, a trait that would certainly have appealed to Ravel. He had not studied at the Conservatoire, had never competed for the Prix de Rome, and had produced no symphonies and no operas. His accession to a professorial chair had long been resisted: in 1892 the director, Ambroise Thomas, had refused to appoint him to the position left vacant by the death of Ernest Guiraud ('Fauré? Never! If he comes I go!'[34]). By 1896, however, it was Thomas who had gone – he died that January – and when Jules Massenet announced his retirement the new director, Théodore Dubois, appointed Fauré to take over his composition class.

For Fauré, at least, Ravel was an assiduous student – 'very intelligent, very gifted', reads his examination report from January 1899 – although he also found the young composer 'too recherché, too refined'. In the June examinations he was 'still unfocused in his intentions, which for now are rather chaotic'. Nevertheless, Fauré added drily, 'he's beginning to calm down'; six months later he reported a 'notable increase in maturity'.[35] Ravel flourished in the liberal, exploratory atmosphere of Fauré's class, forging a deep and affectionate admiration for his teacher and lifelong friendships with his classmates, among whom were Charles Koechlin, Florent Schmitt, George Enescu and Émile Vuillermoz. Roland-Manuel later described the class as the musician's equivalent of Mallarmé's famous *mardis*: a place defined by 'the particular charm of free conversation, where the secrets of art slipped in, where the laws of sensitive appreciation gently offered themselves to the ears, without imposing themselves dogmatically on the spirit'.[36] Ravel took particular delight in recalling how he had once brought a new piece to class (possibly a movement of his String Quartet), to find it rejected decisively by his teacher. A few days later, however, Fauré asked Ravel to bring it back to him. 'Why do you wish to see that again, *maître*? Is it not a failure?', Ravel asked. 'I might have been wrong,' Fauré replied.[37]

Fauré's students were also the beneficiaries of his diplomatic acumen, and his access and influence within the complex networks of the Parisian salons. It was through his teacher that Ravel was introduced to the *vendredis* of Marguerite de Saint-Marceaux (universally known as Meg), which were renowned for their discriminating audiences. 'He is an original artist, but excessively mannered,' Meg recorded in her diary after Ravel's first visit, on 1 April 1898.[38] On 20 August Ravel wrote to Meg from Granville in Normandy (where he was employed for the summer as pianist at the casino), offering her his newest song, the Leconte de Lisle setting *Chanson du rouet*:

> The little symbolist, most happy that you have deigned to take notice of his music, offers the liveliest regrets for not having perpetrated another new song recently. Some might believe him to be overwhelmed with remorse. Sadly, he is nothing of the sort: he is incorrigible, and quite ready to continue in the same vein [. . .] He will take the liberty of sending you his latest composition, which is at least two months old, and which, by chance, might prove singable.[39]

One of Ravel's earliest documented letters, this is also a thoroughly uncharacteristic missive, its florid, mock-deprecatory flattery utterly divorced from his usual economical frankness. It suggests a composer, and a man, still trying out new ways of being, uncertain of his reception and grasping for an individual voice.

In an essay published in the collection *Maurice Ravel par quelques-uns de ses familiers* (1939), the writer Colette would recall encountering Ravel *chez* Meg: 'perhaps secretly shy, Ravel maintained an aloof air, a dry manner [. . .] I remember no particular conversation with him, no gesture of friendship.'[40] Colette's sketch precedes – and seems to clear the way for – the volume's next essay, by the poet Tristan Klingsor. 'Slender but sturdy, outwardly facetious and yet secretly determined', Klingsor wrote, Ravel 'seemed mysterious because he was too reserved to reveal his deep passion. A touch of humour helped him to mask it.'[41] Like Viñes in 1896, Klingsor could see past the insouciance to the anxiety and self-doubt that haunted Ravel in his mid-twenties. Colette, noting his predilection for bold ties, wrote that he seemed to seek attention, yet 'feared criticism'.[42] Klingsor explained that 'this ambitious dream-carrier loved to appear obsessed by the external. He took pleasure in presenting himself as a dandy. With the most serious air in the world, he would display his ties and his socks for admiration, and gravely discuss their colour.' But, he adds, 'I'd smile.'[43]

Alongside his studies with Gedalge and Fauré, Ravel was pursuing a vigorous programme of private musical exploration with Viñes. While they eagerly surveyed Franck's *Les Éolides*, Chabrier's *La Sulamite* and Debussy's *Proses lyriques*, they were drawn above all to Russian orchestral repertoire. Like Debussy, Ravel found in the music of the Mighty Handful a vivid alternative to the Germanic tradition. He was profoundly influenced by the chromatic and modal fluency of the Russians, their concern with naturalistic text-setting and kaleidoscopic orchestration – although he preferred the rougher edges and bold harmonic contours of Musorgsky to Rimsky-Korsakov's rich perfections.

One afternoon in May 1898, Ravel arrived with a new, Russian-tinted work of his own: 'an overture, *Shéhérazade*, which he and

[Lucien] Garban [a Conservatoire classmate, and later Ravel's house editor at Durand] played for me as a duet. We drank absinthe, me for the first time in my life,' Viñes recorded, perhaps a little dazedly.[44] In his 'Autobiographical Sketch' Ravel would describe this 'ouverture de féerie' as a literal overture for an 'unfinished, unpublished' opera based on the *Mille et une nuits* (1704–12) of Antoine Galland. No trace remains of anything more than the overture, however; after completing it, Ravel appears to have moved on to other projects. (By late 1898 he was planning an opera, *Olympia*, on E.T.A. Hoffmann's 'Der Sandmann', although nothing came of that either.)

Shéhérazade was premiered at the SNM on 27 May 1899, with Ravel himself conducting. While it met with some applause, there was also much whistling (expressing vigorous disapproval). Viñes recorded that he had stood to applaud, 'crying "bravo, bravo" and clapping as hard as I could, so that everyone was compelled to notice me. Truly Ravel deserves it because he has such talent and he is young and totally unknown.'[45] The reviews were not kind. Henri Gauthier-Villars ('Willy') labelled the work 'Rimsky fiddled with by a *debussyste*'; 'out of charity,' he wrote snidely, 'I will redact the name of this mediocrely gifted debutant.'[46] In later years Ravel unhesitatingly admitted that *Shéhérazade* was 'poorly conceived, and full of whole-tone scales. There were so many, in fact, that I was put off them for life.'[47] He never sought to publish the overture, or to have it performed again.

In the spring of 1900 Ravel made the first of an eventual five attempts for the Prix de Rome. Awarded by the Académie des Beaux-Arts, the prize (previously held by composers including Berlioz, Gounod, Bizet and Debussy) entitled the winner to a period of funded composition, beginning with two years' residence at the Villa Médicis in Rome. Ravel prepared himself by setting the cantata *Callirhoé* (the prescribed text for the prize in 1899), which he presented for the Conservatoire examinations in January 1900. He then produced a fugue and a chorus (*Les Bayadères*) for the *concours d'essai* (preliminary round) but was excluded from the *concours définitif* (final round), the prize going to his classmate and friend Florent Schmitt.

Competitors for the Prix de Rome at the Château de Compiègne, 1900. The eventual winner, Florent Schmitt, perches on the back of the bench (back row, second from left). Ravel is seated, at right, in bowler hat and long coat.

This episode left Ravel acutely conscious of his growing distance from the musical 'establishment'. He wrote frustratedly to another classmate, Dumitru Kiriac, of *Callirhoé*, that he

> was really counting on it to have an impact: rather grey music, prudently passionate, with a boldness that the gentlemen of the Institut would be able to comprehend. As for the orchestration, Gedalge found it deft and elegant. But all that was a flop. Although Fauré tried to plead for me, Monsieur Dubois told him that he was deceiving himself about my musical gifts. What worries me is that these criticisms were directed, not at my cantata, but, indirectly, at *Shéhérazade* – you will recall that the Director [Dubois] was present at the first performance. Will I have to contend with the fallout for the next five years?[48]

In July 1900 Ravel presented himself for the Conservatoire's end-of-year examinations. Once again, he won no honours, a third successive failure that resulted in him being formally banished from Fauré's class. Twenty-five years old, he had now been twice dismissed from the Conservatoire and had fallen at the first hurdle of the Prix de Rome. His first two showings at the SNM had been disastrous; a third, in January 1900 (*Deux épigrammes de Clément Marot*), had prompted no outrage but – almost as discouraging – failed to raise more than a flicker of attention in the musical press: 'agreeable and nothing more', wrote Gauthier-Villars.[49]

But Fauré, whose advocacy had secured the premiere of *Shéhérazade*, had not given up on his wayward pupil. In September 1900 he sent Ravel a letter of warm reassurance, tacitly acknowledging his frustration and disappointment, and making it clear that he would be welcomed back to Fauré's composition class as an auditor, regardless of his 'official' status at the Conservatoire: 'October is approaching, and will see us reunited [. . .] I hope that you will bring us all the excellent things that you can offer, gifted as you are. Perhaps you've written a little over the vacation?'[50] He also offered generous praise for a piece Ravel had composed some eighteen months earlier, and which had recently been published by the firm of Demets: 'I was very happy to receive your *Pavane*, which I like enormously.' Fauré was not alone. *Pavane pour une Infante défunte* was Ravel's first true success, its assured pianism, attractive melody and fashionably 'antique' textures ensuring its rapid assimilation in the salons. The title Ravel claimed to have devised purely for its pleasing assonances and rhythms; like Fauré's own *Pavane* of 1887, it was never intended to be funereal. 'I wrote a Pavane for a dead Princess, not a dead Pavane for a Princess,' he later remarked to the pianist and writer Charles Oulmont.[51]

Steeling his nerve, in 1901 Ravel entered once again for the Prix de Rome, this time passing successfully through the *concours d'essai* and competing for the first time in the *concours définitif*. From the Villa Médicis, Schmitt kept up a flow of encouraging letters. 'A nice simple chorus [. . .] with none of these Chinese scales,' he cautioned, remembering the ill-fated 'exotic' turns of *Les Bayadères*;

and, for the cantata, 'moderation above all [. . .] it should be clear and comprehensible on a first hearing, without being banal.' When Ravel came away with the '2ᵉ second grand prix' (effectively the third prize) for his cantata *Myrrha*, Schmitt sent praise and encouragement, noting that Ravel had done well to counteract the negative impressions not just of his initial failure but of *Shéhérazade* and *Sites auriculaires*: 'At the very least, they will look favourably on you next year, and it won't take you four years to erase a bad first impression, as it did me.'[52]

In a 1926 interview Ravel would call *Myrrha* a 'cantate parodique', while Roland-Manuel ascribed to its 'slow waltz[es] and swooning melodies' a 'complacent skill not always very far removed from ironic pastiche'.[53] If these later reflections doubtless contain an element of apologism, they hint at something more fundamental, too. Conscientiously embroidering his first *concours* cantata with threads of Massenet, Gounod and Saint-Saëns, Ravel had tried, and not quite succeeded, to adopt a manner that was not his own. But, with his musical language still malleable, his technique not yet entirely in focus, he nevertheless came closer to success in 1901 than he ever would again. Over the four years that followed, with his increasing mastery came a clarity and confidence of purpose, bolstered by the support and artistic sympathy of such friends as Klingsor and Schmitt. When Ravel returned to 'Classical' idioms, in his String Quartet and *Sonatine*, it would be with the deliberation of a composer who now understood just what he could make of them. And when, more than two decades later, he embraced and declared a parade of 'models' in *L'Enfant et les sortilèges* – from Monteverdi to Massenet and music hall – it was with complete awareness of where the line between pastiche and homage could be drawn.

2
Agent provocateur

On 30 June 1902 Marguerite de Saint-Marceaux wrote in her journal, 'Ravel didn't win the Prix de Rome. [Roger-]Ducasse was second.'[1] That terse record – Meg didn't bother mentioning Aymé Kunc, who *did* win – encapsulates the expectations and tensions that encircled Ravel after 1901. Through his unsuccessful jousts at the Prix de Rome and further tangles with the Conservatoire, he continued to be dogged by accusations of tasteless provocation and simple incompetence. Yet by 1903 he was serving on the committee of the SNM. Performances began to come; he took on pupils, received some useful commissions and embarked on works of greater scope and ambition: amused curiosity and offended conservatism began to be balanced, in the press, by grudging respect, faint praise and even, in some quarters, enthusiastic advocacy. It became increasingly clear that Ravel's was a voice that could not be ignored, although it might be loudly shouted down.

One of the catalysts for that shift, wholly unprompted by Ravel himself, occurred two months before Meg's journal entry: on 30 April 1902 Debussy's opera *Pelléas et Mélisande* opened at the Opéra-Comique de Paris. *Pelléas* was a cultural watershed. Probed, reviled, parodied, venerated and valorized, it swiftly permeated the fabric of French musical discourse. It was followed by a series of landmark works: the piano *Estampes* and *Images*, the song triptychs *Fêtes galantes* and, in October 1905, the 'three symphonic sketches' of *La Mer*. By the time those sweeping seascapes received their first performance, Debussy had come to occupy an unassailable position in the narratives of French art and creative thought. He and his opera had become the standard against which all emerging composers were judged, and a measure of the changing times.

In the spring of 1901 Ravel collaborated with his friends Raoul Bardac and Lucien Garban to produce two-piano transcriptions of Debussy's orchestral *Nocturnes*, with Ravel tackling the third movement, 'Sirènes'. That task brought him, for the first time, into Debussy's circle: 'Cher Monsieur', Debussy wrote to him in April 1901, but by June he had become 'Cher ami'.[2] For the next three years their relations were cordial if not intimate, sufficiently close that Debussy would be invited to a pre-premiere rehearsal of Ravel's String Quartet on 4 March 1904. Three months after that, however, Debussy left his wife, Lilly, for Emma Bardac (mother of Raoul), a very public scandal that was compounded when Lilly subsequently attempted suicide. Ravel joined a number of colleagues in contributing to a fund to support her, a gesture that seems not to have passed unnoticed by Debussy (who broke with a number of friends during this turbulent period). No further direct correspondence between the two men can be traced.

More potent than this personal complication was the growing professional one. As Ravel's reputation grew, his name was continually yoked with Debussy's. The more confident and individual he became, the more polemical were the critics – and from some quarters, the more strident grew the cries of *debussysme*, of imitation and even, eventually, of plagiarism. That both composers chafed at this situation is clear from their respective correspondence, although they remained intensely interested in each other's musical discoveries: Viñes was several times asked to play new works by one composer to the other. It was only decades later, though, that Ravel would be able to acknowledge Debussy's role in his own development. Hélène Jourdan-Morhange described him, late in life, overwhelmed with emotion by a radio broadcast of *Prélude à l'après-midi d'un faune*: 'It was in listening to *L'Après-midi* for the first time that I understood what music was.'[3]

Even before the premiere of *Pelléas*, the murmurs of *debussysme* had begun. On 5 April 1902 Viñes gave the official premiere, at

Ricardo Viñes and Ravel, 1905.

the SNM, of Ravel's *Pavane pour une Infante défunte* and *Jeux d'eau*. Reviewing the concert, the critic Pierre Lalo noted an improvement on the 'incoherence and disorder' of 'a certain *Shéhérazade*', but found the style somewhat derivative, perceiving the influence not just of Chabrier, but 'still more often that of Debussy' – an allegation that Ravel was later firmly to refute.[4] Yet the experience of transcribing 'Sirènes' had marked Ravel more than he allowed. 'Perhaps the most perfectly beautiful', he had written to Florent Schmitt, it was also 'undoubtedly the most perilous' of Debussy's *Nocturnes*: not just the longest movement, but that in which texture and timbre are imbued most profoundly with structural function (it is the only one of the three movements to include a wordless chorus).[5] The pianistic experimentation and compositional engagement demanded by such a transcription indisputably flowed into *Jeux d'eau*, which was composed in the autumn of 1901, and whose individuality and innovation lie in its fusion of figuration and architecture. The shimmering textures of Ravel's musical fountains are not adjectival but syntactic; not a vehicle for the musical material, but its very essence.

The epigraph to *Jeux d'eau* ('Dieu fluvial riant de l'eau qui le chatouille' – 'River god laughing as the water tickles him') is drawn from Henri de Régnier's poem 'Fête d'eau', one of a collection of sonnets extolling the fountains of Versailles. Ravel perhaps had that text directly from Régnier himself, for it was published only in 1902 (in the collection *La Cité des eaux*), and one of the three surviving autographs of *Jeux d'eau* shows the epigraph added in the poet's hand. When and how Ravel had come to meet Régnier – a decade older and already recognized as one of the most distinguished writers of his day – is nowhere recorded, although Tristan Klingsor is the most likely point of contact. While Ravel and Viñes had admired Régnier's poetry since the mid-1890s, Ravel would set it just once, in the song *Les grands vents venus d'outre-mer* (1907).

By December 1902 Ravel had also completed the Scherzo of his String Quartet. This was followed a month later by the opening *Allegro moderato*, which he submitted for a Conservatoire composition prize. Once again, he found himself unhappily at odds with the institution: Paul Ladmirault recalled casting an 'indiscreet' glance over the judges' shoulders and noticing that one had labelled Ravel's quartet simply 'pénible' (difficult, or impossible).[6] In what was possibly some kind of institutional record, Ravel was expelled from the Conservatoire a third time, now banned even from auditing Fauré's class.

Undeterred by this final stinging break, by April 1903 Ravel had finished his quartet. His first completed work in one of the great 'traditional' genres, it was also the most sustained and thoughtful dialogue he had yet mounted with musical history. The sonata form of the first movement is articulated with Classical precision; indeed, the presentation of the first subject, across four regular four-bar phrases, is Mozartian in its textural clarity (if not its harmonic logic). Nevertheless, as the movement progresses Ravel's distinctive interventions become increasingly apparent. As with *Jeux d'eau* (which plays on oppositions of the semitone and tritone), the harmonic argument is not between two established tonal areas: the first and second subjects, respectively in F and a modal D minor, sit within the same diatonic envelope. Rather, the drama of the movement lies in the contrasts between those broadly stable passages and the chromatic and octatonic writing that waylays the development, the harmonic colours of the Russian orchestral works Ravel loved setting in glowing relief the contours of the Classical form.

The fleet-footed Scherzo, in A minor, opens with the first violin tracing the same upward fifth (a' to e'') as the first movement's second subject. This fleeting recollection, however, is quickly swept away in a complex dance of cross-rhythms, accentuated by the virtuosic play of *pizzicato* and *arco* textures. The slower Trio theme, although based loosely in a modal G minor, melodically echoes the very first phrase of the quartet, circling outwards from a' towards an upper- and lower-octave D. The slow movement begins with a more meditative exploration of that same opening theme, which is then recalled explicitly in the two brief *Très calme* passages. The *Vif et agacé* finale upends the first movement's metric regularity by setting the same motif in quintuple metre.

These cyclic games reflect a more recent strand of compositional inheritance, as transmitted through the chamber music of Franck as well as Debussy's String Quartet of 1893. Ravel would note in his 'Autobiographical Sketch' that his quartet responded to 'a passion for musical form'. Its architectural ingenuity lies in the fusion of the Viennese tradition with the French, Mozartian lucidity reimagined with French *clarté*.

Premiered at the SNM on 5 March 1904, the String Quartet received a warmer public reception and a more extensive, thoughtful and broadly positive critical response than any Ravel had yet experienced. The progressive critic Louis Laloy called it 'the work of a sensitive and gifted musician, steeped in feeling, clarity and harmony', while Michel-Dmitri Calvocoressi drew attention to Ravel's originality and his 'remarkable feeling for purity of line and architectural balance'.[7] Even Pierre Lalo considered certain passages 'very pleasant to listen to', although much of his column in *Le Temps* was devoted to what was rapidly becoming his primary thesis: that Ravel was the leading representative of a younger generation whose obsession with the music of Debussy was driving them to follow blindly in the older composer's footsteps. 'In its harmony,' Lalo wrote,

> in its chord progressions, in its sonority, in its form, in every single respect and in every sensation it evokes, there is an extraordinary resemblance to the music of M. Debussy [. . .] This is the evil I spoke of; this is the epidemic that is upon us. For M. Ravel, if his example is the most remarkable and the most striking, is far from alone.[8]

In the *Mercure de France*, however, Jean Marnold took up this point with more subtlety and insight. While he noted a surface kinship with Debussy, he stressed that 'on examination, one realizes that this is filiation, not pastiche.' This review, from a critic of seriousness and distinction, must have been among the most satisfying Ravel had yet received. Describing the quartet as 'a work of rich and powerful musicality', Marnold praised its 'limpid form' and 'delightfully original eloquence [. . .] We must remember the name of Maurice Ravel. He is one of the masters of tomorrow.'[9]

Ravel might have taken particular pleasure in Marnold's opening sally: 'When one has heard Ravel's Quartet in F, one is no longer surprised that the blockheads of the Institut have refused him the Prix de Rome.' In the spring of 1903 Ravel had tackled a third competition cantata, *Alyssa*, armed with a twist of 'hangman's rope' that his Basque 'cousin' Jane Gaudin had sent to bring him luck.[10] Once again, however, he had been unsuccessful, the prize going to Raoul Laparra. But 'even Laparra, despite his triumph, won't have a good memory of it,' Ravel wrote to Gaudin: Fauré – Laparra's teacher as well as Ravel's – had declared that the judgement was 'scandalous' and 'patently predetermined'. Meanwhile, Ravel had offered to divide the hangman's rope between the performers of his cantata in gratitude – 'but what do you think? None of them wanted it!!!'[11]

However dispiriting, this fourth failure was cushioned by more than a healthy dose of cynicism. Comfort could be found in the satisfying proof of the String Quartet – a new work far more important than *Alyssa*, and one whose dedication 'À mon cher maître Gabriel Fauré' must, by the summer of 1903, have felt more fitting than ever. Moreover, Ravel could now find solace in a supportive and intensely knowledgeable company of friends, among whom he could let down his defences and allow himself to feel part of an ambitious whole. In 1904 he didn't bother competing for the Prix de Rome.

Coalescing between 1902 and 1904, Ravel's artistic circle initially comprised Viñes and the critics Calvocoressi and Émile Vuillermoz, together with the painter Paul Sordes and the poets Léon-Paul Fargue and Klingsor. By January 1904 Viñes was writing that their gatherings 'included many new people'. The new arrivals included Déodat de Séverac and Maurice Delage, the latter an aspiring composer who soon became Ravel's student and lifelong friend.[12] 'I had just been admitted to an exclusive circle whose enthusiasm and spirit of unity would mark me profoundly,' Delage recalled in 1939. 'Ravel naturally seemed to be the centre of this circle, which as yet had no name.'[13]

The name was not long in coming. Surging up the rue de Rome one evening they collided with a newspaper seller, who cried out, 'Attention! Les Apaches!' Viñes was entranced with the word – more commonly used to describe gangs of hooligans – and the group immediately claimed it.[14] They also adopted a call sign, the opening of Borodin's Symphony no. 2 (which might be whistled, for example, to locate fellow Apaches among the crowds in a theatre foyer), and an imaginary personage, 'Gomez de Riquet', to whom a prior engagement could be pleaded when refusing an unwelcome invitation.

The Apaches met regularly on Saturday evenings, first at Sordes' studio, then – as the size and volume of the gatherings increased – in a detached house Delage acquired in the suburb of Auteuil. But the flow of ideas and conversation soon became almost continuous: 'each of us knew, each of us understood, day by day, what the others were thinking and doing,' wrote Fargue.[15] They would meet before concerts and after them and, fortified by a *cornet* of tobacco, would walk and talk for hours through the nocturnal streets. They developed their own slang, their in-jokes and codes, and – like any circle of close friends – they took care of one another, staying up all night to copy orchestral parts, or helping to deal with the practicalities of bereavements.

Although he had been banished from Fauré's Conservatoire class, Ravel found among the Apaches a workshop no less congenial and markedly more adventurous. The absence of society formalities permitted discussion and experimentation far more uninhibited than in the salons. Fargue particularly recalled Ravel 'playing us the latest version of his String Quartet, section by section and draft by draft, as the work developed', while Viñes's journal mentions various pieces that never reached completion.[16] Much other new music was played and discussed, too, with Debussy featuring heavily (they were devoted *Pelléastres*), along with the Russians.

On 7 November 1903 the Apaches enjoyed a two-piano rendering of Glazunov's *Fantaisie orientale* paired with three new songs by Ravel, settings of poems from Klingsor's just-published collection *Shéhérazade*.[17] Unlike Galland's *Mille et une nuits*, Klingsor's

A gathering of the Apaches *chez* Florent Schmitt, 1910, probably photographed by Pierre Haour. Back row, left to right: Paul Sordes, Florent Schmitt, Léon-Paul Fargue, Jeanne Schmitt; middle: Jeanne Haour, 'Raton' Schmitt, Léon Pivet; front: Roger Haour, Ravel, Jeanne and Christine Pivet.

Shéhérazade depicts an Orient that is imagined but never grasped. 'Asie' (the first of Ravel's texts) paints a series of scenes the poet would *like* to see, which he dreams not so much of experiencing as of *recounting*. This sinuous refraction of the real and the imagined is conjured in the subtle opposition of pitch centres. At figure 2 the pitch d^1, maintained through the introductory bars 7–10 ('vieux pays merveilleux . . .' – 'ancient, wondrous land') effectively splits to E♭ and D♭, via the E-flat minor-seventh harmony that underpins the first part of the catalogue of marvels. That harmony is regained at the song's climax (fig. 15), before giving way again to octave Ds at figure 16, prefiguring the vocal return to d^1 for the final line of the poem ('And then, later to return and retell my adventures to those intrigued by dreams . . .'). As the lush textures contract to that sparse pedal note, the artful narration is revealed as the only 'real' experience.

In 1939 Vuillermoz would describe 'Asie' as a response to Baudelaire's 'L'Invitation au voyage'.[18] Klingsor himself answered

Baudelaire more directly in another poem in his collection, 'Le Voyage' (whose title mirrors the last poem of *Les Fleurs du mal*). 'But no, better off staying here', 'Le Voyage' begins firmly, ending with the admission 'For the fantasy is finer than reality/ For the finest lands are those that one knows not,/ And the finest voyage is that made in dream.' (When Charles Koechlin set that poem in 1922, he neatly quoted the opening of Ravel's 'Asie' in his own first bar.) It was doubtless Klingsor's poetic distance, with its touch of knowing irony and its nods to Baudelaire, that allowed Ravel to revisit this tale-of-tales, the echoes of Rimsky-Korsakov now fainter and better assimilated into an increasingly individual command of musical architecture and orchestration.

Klingsor's *Shéhérazade* had itself emerged in part through the musical explorations of the Apaches: another of its poems, 'Les Djinns', evokes 'the djinns of the Orient', who lie concealed in the flourishes of Rimsky-Korsakov's baton. In July 1904, a few weeks after the soprano Jeanne Hatto gave the formal premiere of Ravel's *Shéhérazade* at the SNM, Viñes and Ravel completed the circle by playing Rimsky's *Scheherazade* in duet reduction at a gathering of the Apaches. Viñes rounded off the evening with Balakirev's diabolically difficult *Islamey*, Debussy's newly published *Estampes* and Chopin's Étude op. 10, no. 6.[19] Three months later, on 15 October, Ravel arrived in Auteuil with a new piano piece that makes the same unusual modulation as that Étude, from E-flat minor to E major; like the Étude, it is grounded in oscillating chromatic motion around the interval of a second. Ravel dedicated this new piece, 'Oiseaux tristes', to Viñes.

That ascription has long been considered, and doubtless partly was, a wry joke: the least virtuosic of the five scintillating movements Ravel was to title *Miroirs*, 'Oiseaux tristes' would be offered to the finest pianist of the Apaches. But it is typical of the composer that a genuine homage should rest beneath an ironic exterior. Klingsor wrote that Ravel often had little to say at the gatherings of the Apaches: listening 'in stillness, he would compare, analyse internally; even as he assumed an air of doing nothing at all, he was working.'[20] The dedication of 'Oiseaux tristes' perhaps acknowledges that Viñes's performance that night in July had sparked something for the composer, the musico-poetic spiral of *Shéhérazade* unfurling a new arc of inspiration and creative exchange.

Initially, however, 'Oiseaux tristes' met with a bewildered response from Ravel's friends: Viñes described it as 'a new piano piece that pleased nobody but me'.[21] Despite this unencouraging reception, by the spring of 1905 Ravel had completed a companion piece, 'Une barque sur l'océan'. Emerging from the E-flat minor of 'Oiseaux tristes', the modal F-sharp minor/A major tonality of 'Une barque' offers one of the most breathtaking of Ravel's transitions, the oppressive heat of the dark woods dissipating in a gust of fresh sea air. The intensity of expressive contrast, with its flat-side/sharp-side opposition and arpeggio figurations, suggests a direct and pungent (if perhaps unconscious) reminiscence of a similarly spectacular transition in *Pelléas et Mélisande*: at the end of Act III scene 2, Pelléas and Golaud emerge from the vaults into the sunlight and sea breezes, as Pelléas sings, 'Ah! I can breathe at last!'

The eventual first, fourth and fifth of the *Miroirs* probably date from the autumn of 1905, in the months that followed Ravel's return from a cruise on the yacht *Aimée* (discussed below). 'Noctuelles' returns to the Lisztian virtuosity of *Jeux d'eau*, while 'Alborada del gracioso' – whose title Ravel later translated as 'Aubade de bouffon' ('Morning song of the clown') – exploits a more flamboyant physicality, the finger-shredding double glissandi and repeated notes recalling *Islamey*. If its exuberant Spanishness represents a confident reimagining of the early *Sérénade grotesque*, 'La Vallée des cloches' returns to the sonorities of 'Entre cloches'. Ravel reportedly claimed that this final movement evoked the midday bells of the churches of Paris, but the sonorous experiences of his summer cruise were perhaps still resonating, too: 'first impression of Holland: cathedrals and bells in the night', he had written to Delage from Maastricht, later describing an excursion accompanied by 'a sempiternal carillon'.[22]

In his account of Ravel's first playing of his 'Oiseaux tristes', Delage writes that in the 'moment of silence' that followed, Fargue began 'rummaging in his pockets, pulled out a piece of paper, and announced, "Of course, it's not finished yet". Then in his gaunt voice, he painted for us "La petite gare aux ombres courtes, lasse de cinq heures" ["The small, short-shadowed station, in its five o'clock weariness"].'[23] That poem, from a 1903–4 collection then titled *Nocturnes*, continues to the lines 'Les noctuelles des hangars partent, d'un vol gauche, cravater d'autres poutres' ('from their barns the night moths launch themselves, in ungainly flight, to circle around other beams') – an image that Vuillermoz was to claim as the direct inspiration for 'Noctuelles'.[24] Paul Roberts has astutely noted several other echoes of Fargue's *Nocturnes* in the titles of Ravel's *Miroirs*: one poem sketches 'un oiseau triste', whose song is preceded by 'a piano, slowly musing'; another evokes a laden 'barque' making its way towards the shore.[25] Like Klingsor's *Shéhérazade*, Fargue's *Nocturnes* may themselves owe a debt to the conversations of the Apaches: five of the poems were initially inscribed to members of the group (if not to Ravel himself).[26] Ravel in turn would offer his *Miroirs* to five of the Apaches, the dedications highlighting their eclectic creative languages: poet (Fargue), pianist (Viñes), painter (Sordes), musicologist-critic (Calvocoressi) and composer (Delage). Perhaps surprisingly, he would set Fargue's poetry just once, almost a quarter of a century later, in the enigmatic little song *Rêves* (1927).

By the beginning of 1905 the Apaches had adopted a third headquarters, at the home of Cipa and Ida Godebski. Cipa, who had known Viñes since the mid-1890s, was a passionate and knowledgeable musical amateur from an intensely cultured Polish family. Ravel soon counted the Godebskis among his closest friends, becoming a favourite uncle to their young children Mimi and Jean. He also made the acquaintance of Cipa's half-sister Misia Natanson (later Edwards, then Sert), who was one of the great animating spirits of the Belle Époque, and whose artistic sympathy and unmatchable connections were to be a source of moral and practical support for the composer over the next two decades. Between Natanson – who married the newspaper magnate Alfred Edwards in 1905 – and the Apaches, by the time he celebrated his thirtieth

Ravel as sketched by Léon-Paul Fargue, *c.* 1902.

birthday, Ravel's immediate circle had come to provide much more than comradeship and inspiration. 'Thus we saw Ravel's career take shape, its trajectory ever more clearly determined,' Fargue wrote many years later.[27] But his friends were more than bystanders: their advocacy in the press and through the city's musical networks would play a key role in determining that trajectory. And at no time would Ravel need them more than in the spring of 1905.

Early in 1904 the Ravel family had moved out to the suburb of Levallois, doubtless to spare Pierre-Joseph a wearing commute to the family business. Now in his seventies and increasingly frail, Ravel's father, assisted by Édouard, was nevertheless mounting his firm's most ambitious enterprise yet. On 27 November 1903 father and son had filed a patent for a device they called 'Le Tourbillon de la Mort' (the Whirlwind of Death): a stunt vehicle that, when launched from a ramp, was capable of turning a somersault metres in the air. In early 1905 the Casino de Paris paid 25,000 francs for a mere two months' exclusive rights to the machine, and on 22 March the Tourbillon de la Mort made a stunning début. 'Offers of engagements are coming in from all sides, especially from America. Perhaps this will make our fortunes! It could not come too soon for my father, I must say,' Ravel wrote excitedly to Jane Gaudin.[28] But on 14 April disaster struck. Completing its somersault, the vehicle seemed to land awkwardly. The driver, a young woman named Marcelle Randal, was carried out unconscious, and the next day she died.

Over the next few weeks the Parisian papers were full of the tragedy and the subsequent investigation. Columnists fulminated; one member of the Municipal Council of Paris gave a passionate speech decrying the extremes to which the desire for 'entertainment' had led a voracious public; and 250 young women presented themselves to the Casino as potential replacement drivers. 'Impossible, you'll understand, to leave Paris just now,' Ravel wrote to Gaudin on 24 April: 'Papa and Édouard are before the magistrate as I write!!'[29] On 5 May the magistrate charged both Ravels, Randal's manager and the directors of the Casino with manslaughter. The next day, the choruses and fugues for the *concours d'essai* of the Prix de Rome were presented at Compiègne.

This year Ravel was competing once more, in the knowledge that it was his last opportunity, the prize being open only to unmarried composers under the age of thirty. It was also his best chance yet, since two first prizes were available, the 1904 winner having abandoned his tenure in Rome to get married. Moreover, the composer of the String Quartet, *Shéhérazade* and *Jeux d'eau* was as accomplished a candidate as the competition had seen in years.

The progressive *Mercure musical* welcomed Ravel's entry by declaring that 'all our best wishes go with him'; its failure to mention any of the eighteen other candidates was an unsubtle reminder of the weight of expectation that lay upon him.[30]

On 13 May the six contenders for the *concours définitif* were announced. Ravel was not among them. All the successful candidates, in fact, were pupils of Charles Lenepveu – the only one of the three Conservatoire composition professors who, as a member of the Institut de France, was eligible to serve on the jury. This obvious skewing of the field, and the apparently incomprehensible decision to exclude Ravel, set off a firestorm in the musical press. On 21 May the newspaper *Le Matin* – owned by Edwards – ran a scathing article demanding to know how a candidate who had previously attained a second *grand prix* could be considered so incompetent as not to progress to the *concours définitif*. Offered a right of response, Lenepveu said bluntly that he 'didn't make the rules, and it's not my fault that I'm a member of the Institut'.

The next day *Le Matin* ran an interview with Ravel, who condemned his exclusion in terms of the insult offered to his teacher. 'Are not MM. Widor and Fauré sufficiently capable of teaching fugue, counterpoint and composition?' he asked: '[their] artistic worth and professional integrity cannot be doubted.' On 26 May the distinguished scholar and dramatist Romain Rolland joined the fray: 'I'm not a friend of Ravel's; indeed, I can say that I have little personal sympathy for his subtle, refined art. But justice compels me to say that Ravel is not just a promising student: he is already one of the leading masters of our younger school.' What was the point of the whole enterprise, Rolland asked, 'if it continues to close the doors to such remarkable artists, of such originality; to a man such as Ravel, [who] comes to the [Prix de Rome] not as a student, but as a *composer*?'[31]

As the furore deepened, on 22 May Pierre-Joseph and Édouard Ravel were again before the magistrate, this time armed with a small working model of their machine to argue 'energetically' (as *Le Radical* reported on 24 May) that it presented 'no danger whatsoever'. The next day *Le Matin* followed its series of articles

Lawyers examine Pierre-Joseph Ravel's model of Le Tourbillon de la Mort, *Le Matin*, 23 May 1905.

vigorously defending Ravel with a column impugning his father and brother, asserting that Édouard had compelled Randal to perform despite her obvious indisposition, because 'the public is waiting!' As the hearings continued, however, it became clear that while witnesses offered different accounts of the fatal landing, the vehicle itself was essentially undamaged: there had been no 'crash'. The medical evidence also became increasingly complicated, with various experts, including Randal's own physician, testifying that the unfortunate driver had been suffering from acute nephritis as well as tuberculosis (an autopsy revealed serious lung damage), and possibly a heart condition and anaemia as well; several witnesses testified that she appeared to have lost consciousness before the fatal leap. At the end of May all five defendants were acquitted.

The jury that determined Maurice Ravel's fate, meanwhile, had some justification for condemning him. His chorus, *L'Aurore*, might sound more confidently 'Ravelian' than any of his previous Prix de Rome essays – the orchestral prelude alone, with its *pianissimo* horns, *divisi* strings and shimmering high winds, could almost be a fragment of *Daphnis et Chloé* – but it also includes passages of blatant parallel motion. Worse still, Ravel's fugue ends, like *Jeux d'eau*, on the uncompromising dissonance of the major seventh. Such deliberate 'faults', however characteristic, could not be overlooked: to accept such an entry would have necessitated a reconfiguration of the whole competition. Why, then, did Ravel offer such deliberate provocation? Did he decide (as Roger Nichols suggests) that between the trauma of the Tourbillon de la Mort and Pierre-Joseph's failing health, he could not in good conscience leave his family to spend two years in Rome?[32] At a more fundamental level, Ravel had surely recognized that the tension between his increasingly assured and individual language and the demands of the establishment could no longer be resolved. The gauntlet was thrown down: take the parallel motion and major seventh or leave them; he was done with dissembling.

One lasting impact of the *affaire Ravel* was not just profound but revolutionary. In early March Théodore Dubois had announced that he would retire at the end of the academic year, and Lenepveu had been widely tipped to succeed him as director of the Paris Conservatoire. The disastrous Prix de Rome, however, rendered Lenepveu's candidacy untenable, and on 15 June Fauré was announced as Dubois's successor, to the delighted astonishment of his students and friends. On taking up his post that autumn, Fauré – deaf to the outraged squawks of the conservative establishment – would quickly implement a sweeping programme of administrative and curriculum reform, so radical that it prompted a near-rebellion among the professoriate and earned him the nickname 'Robespierre'.

As the twin storms of the Prix de Rome and the Tourbillon de la Mort swirled around him, Ravel was feverishly executing a commission. He had been invited by Alfred and Misia Edwards to join them on their yacht, *Aimée*, for a cruise through the waterways of northern France, Belgium, Holland and Germany. Before departing, however, he had to finish a septet for harp, flute, clarinet and string quartet. In 1904 Debussy had been commissioned by the firm of Pleyel to write a work (*Danse sacrée et danse profane*) showcasing the capabilities of the Pleyel chromatic harp. Ravel's beguiling *Introduction et Allegro* was written at the behest of the rival manufacturer Érard in order to assert the superiority of its pedal harp. The obvious parallels between the contest of instruments and makers, and that of the composers, would not be lost on the critics when Ravel's piece was premiered in early 1907.

Ravel completed *Introduction et Allegro* in '8 days of relentless work and 3 sleepless nights', his haste so great that he left the manuscript on the counter of the tailor's shop to which he had dashed to buy some suitably elegant yachting wear.[33] Even then he missed the boat, and had to be driven by Delage to join his fellow passengers at Soissons.[34] Once on board, however, Ravel seemed to relax, swiftly and completely. His many letters from *Aimée* are unusually poetic, as he took time not just to describe but to reflect and connect. 'Yesterday, a remarkable experience, as the boat moved down the centre of a canal lined with great trees, straight and regular,' he wrote on 7 June. 'I thought of a French garden, of the great ships of the *grand siècle*, and also of certain illustrations from the novels of Jules Verne.' A few weeks later he described 'the most magnificent spectacle. A lake bounded by mills. In the fields, windmills stretching to the horizon. You finish up feeling yourself an automaton, faced with this mechanical landscape.' His father's son, he broke off another letter because he had glimpsed a 'remarkable and magnificent factory' through his window and had to go up on deck to look more closely.[35] And on 5 July, passing through Ahaus, he mused:

> How can I convey to you the impressions of these castles of cast iron, of these incandescent cathedrals, of the marvellous symphony of conveyer belts, of whistles and great hammer blows that surrounds you. Everywhere, a red sky, dark and blazing. Above, a storm broke. We retreated, utterly soaking, in very different frames of mind. Ida [Godebska], terrified, wanted to cry. So did I, but for joy. What music there is in all this! And I intend to make use of it.[36]

In that remarkable paragraph, with its delight in both the nature and the visceral sonic experience of mechanization, we find a thread of fascination and inspiration that runs the length of Ravel's life and work. The emotional concentration and meticulously balanced syntax, too, are as characteristic of the composer as they are of the correspondent. The rich imagery and tumbling clauses of the first sentence are followed by progressively sharper formulations and a striking emotional reverse ('to cry [. . .] for joy'), while the concluding pivot to blunt, determined action gives a propulsive rhythm to the whole. There is even an echo of Baudelaire, whose 'Salon de 1859' extols the 'paradoxical beauty' of industrial architecture and 'a tumultuous sky, weighted with rage and rancour'.[37] Although possibly unintentional, that fleeting reminiscence illuminates Ravel's essentially Romantic and literary imagination, the wild, nocturnal sublime recast through the lens of industrial modernity.

Disembarking from *Aimée*, Ravel threw himself unreservedly into composition. 'I'm in a productive phase,' he wrote to Godebska, and to Meg de Saint-Marceaux, 'I didn't write two bars the whole time, but I've stored away a multitude of impressions and I hope that this winter is going to be extraordinarily productive. I've never felt so happy to be alive.'[38] His immediate priority was a work whose first movement had been written more than two years previously. In March 1903 the *Weekly Critical Review* had announced a competition for 'the first movement of a Pianoforte Sonate [*sic*] in F sharp minor, not to exceed 75 bars in length.' Anonymized submissions were to be judged by a panel reportedly including Charles-Marie Widor, Vincent d'Indy, Alfred Bruneau, Georges Marty, Paul Vidal and the conductor Camille Chevillard.[39] Ravel's entry was signed 'Verla' – a pseudonym the jury should have had little trouble unravelling.

This first movement of Ravel's *Sonatine* distils his rhythmic wit and structural elan. It begins as if in the middle of a sentence, the initial falling fourth sounding as the answer to an unvoiced thought. That opening gesture sets off a play of phrase-rhythm that spans the movement, infusing the trim sonata form with the liveliness of an intricate round dance. The latter movements take up the falling fourth as a unifying motivic thread: in the eloquent Menuet it forms a shadowy reminiscence, *pianissimo* and *Plus lent*, while in the toccata-like Finale the opening theme is again recalled in the two *tranquille – plus lent* passages. First heard in duple time, the initial phrase is thus recast first in triple, then in quintuple metre, a device that imparts a cyclic coherence while gently teasing out imbalances and ambiguities. Only in the closing bars, where the falling fourths sound *fff* as tolling bells, does the rhythmic tension finally ease.

'The *Sonatine* is finished,' Ravel wrote to Delage a few days after returning to Paris, 'and I'm starting work on the *Symphonie*.'[40] While nothing came of this mooted symphony, which crops up in one or two other letters, then sinks without trace, the *Sonatine* proved a turning point in his career. The acquisition of the rights by the publisher Durand marked the beginning of a long and happy partnership: unquestionably the finest of the Parisian firms, Durand was known for its high editorial standards, probity and progressive outlook. Jacques Durand, who was then poised to assume the directorship of the house from his father, Auguste, would write that 'from the beginning of his editorial career, my father had preferred the younger composers of the day; at the end of his life, he saw a new musical dawn breaking, full of a promise that was, for the most part, fulfilled.'[41]

The winter of 1905–6 was indeed productive. By the end of 1905 Ravel had completed *Miroirs* as well as his first setting of his own poetry, *Noël des jouets*. His gift for expressive description sparkles in this little Christmas *mélodie*, with its onomatopoeia of bleating sheep ('Dont la voix grêle bêle:/ "Noël!"' – 'Whose reedy voices bleat/ Noël!') and glittering angel ornaments ('Qui cliquette en bruits symétriques' – 'Jingling in symmetrical sounds'). 'Ravel knew how to see and to release the essential,' reflected the critic René Dumesnil in 1938, 'and to express it he always found the right word, not only by its precise meaning, but still more by its sonority.'[42]

On 6 January 1906 Viñes gave the first performance of *Miroirs* at the SNM. 'Alborada del gracioso' was encored and Marnold likened the pieces' 'revelatory' impact to that of Schumann's *Kreisleriana*.[43] In Pierre Lalo's column, however, the polemic was turning increasingly personal:

> The most conspicuous of [Ravel's] faults is a strange resemblance to M. Claude Debussy; a resemblance so pronounced and so astonishing that often, when listening to a piece of Ravel's, it seems as if one is hearing a fragment of *Pelléas et Mélisande* [. . .] After Chopin, after Schumann, after Liszt, M. Debussy has created a new manner of writing for the piano, a special style, a distinctive virtuosity [. . .] all the young composers are immediately mirroring him, employing the same methods, writing in the same style.[44]

Ravel, by now thoroughly exasperated, wrote to Lalo to point out that when he had composed *Jeux d'eau* Debussy's only published piano music of note was *Pour le piano*: 'I do not need to tell you of my passionate admiration for [these three pieces], but [. . .] from a *purely pianistic* point of view [they] contained nothing really new.'[45]

But Ravel had little time to brood over the follies of critics, for new compositional projects were now vying with rehearsals, premieres, commissions, revisions and the preparation of scores for publication. *Noël des jouets* was swiftly orchestrated, and performed in both versions by the soprano Jane Bathori, perhaps the finest and certainly the most influential art-song specialist of her generation.[46] April also brought the premiere of three Greek folksong arrangements, produced for a lecture-recital given by Calvocoressi. Joined with two more songs tailored for a similar event two years earlier, they would be published at the end of 1906 as the delightful *Cinq mélodies populaires grecques*. So buoyed was Ravel that he could afford to turn his back on a regular source of income, a series of harmony and composition classes that he had been giving to a group of young ladies. He resigned the post in an uncompromising letter of February 1906, complaining that he had been treated as a 'valet de chambre'. He might sometimes have arrived late to his class, he admitted, but his pupils were always later still.[47]

Three days after that unceremonious departure, Ravel wrote to Marnold that he was working on

> a grand waltz, a sort of homage to the memory of the great Strauss, not Richard, the other one, Johann. You know my deep appreciation for these marvellous rhythms, and that I consider the *joie de vivre* expressed through dance much deeper than that of Franckist puritanism.[48]

Little more was to be heard of this 'grand waltz' for some years, however, for Ravel was soon immersed in a far bigger project: his first serious attempt at an opera. His chosen text was *La Cloche engloutie* (The Sunken Bell), translated and adapted by André-Ferdinand Hérold from Gerhart Hauptmann's play *Die versunkene Glocke*. Diving into his libretto in the early summer of 1906, Ravel was excited and optimistic. 'I've never worked with such intensity,' he wrote to Delage on 12 June. 'It's thrilling to write a work for the theatre! I won't say that it comes all by itself, but that's precisely what's best of all.' By late August he claimed that much of the first act and 'a large part of the 2nd' were drafted: 'You want an opera in 5 acts? You'll have it in 1 week!'[49] However, a few passages of draft are all that survive of *La Cloche engloutie*, to which Ravel would return periodically over the next few years before abandoning in 1914. In some of those surviving sketches the vocal lines betray the imprint of *Pelléas*, with their repeated pitches and gentle echoes of the contours and rhythms of the spoken voice. Elsewhere, though, moments of tortuous chromatic motion show the composer exploring the more uncompromising naturalism of a work that he would tackle – and complete – in the autumn of 1906: the five-song cycle *Histoires naturelles*.

'The direct, clear language and the profound, hidden poetry of Jules Renard's poetry tempted me for a long time,' Ravel said of *Histoires naturelles* in his 'Autobiographical Sketch'. Elsewhere he described Renard's texts as 'delicate, rhythmic, though rhythmic in a completely different way from classical verse'.[50] In the climactic line of 'Le Martin-pêcheur' ('The Kingfisher'), for example – 'Je ne respirais plus, tout fier d'être pris pour un arbre par un martin-pêcheur' ('I held my breath, so proud was I to be taken for a tree by a kingfisher') – the repeated *r*s hold up the flow of text, compelling the performer to match the narrator's breathless tread. Ravel casts this as the most understated of musical climaxes, the *subitement ppp* in bar 15 curtailing the hesitant lyricism of the preceding phrase. Only when it has passed do we recognize it as such: the harmonic rhythm slackens; the narrator relaxes; the bird has flown.

The premiere of *Histoires naturelles*, which took place at the SNM on 12 January 1907, was a predictably rowdy affair. Bathori recalled that her audience was galvanized by the first line of 'Le Martin-pêcheur' to a 'veritable revolt',[51] a memory seemingly confirmed by the critic Auguste Sérieyx:

> The Société nationale is not a Music-Hall: we are certainly not opposed to a certain degree of gentle gaiety, and occasional excursions to the extreme limits of good taste can now and then provoke a discreet smile. But there is a difference between these sorts of little accidents, which can be ascribed to inexperience,

and a systematic attempt at 'bluffing'; and the witty author of these *Histoires naturelles* (that is, Jules Renard) seems himself to have expressed, in his 'Martin-pêcheur', the lesson of the unfortunate buffoonery presented at the concert of 12 January: 'Not a bite, this evening'![52]

Even Fauré was troubled, complaining to Ravel's Conservatoire classmate Louis Aubert, 'I'm very fond of Ravel. But I'm not happy with people setting stuff like that to music.'[53] Debussy was equally baffled. 'Do you truly believe in "humoristic" music?' he asked Louis Laloy, who had devoted an extended and enthusiastic article to Ravel's songs in the *Mercure musical*:

> I agree with you that Ravel could not be more gifted, but what irritates me is his 'conjuror's' attitude, or, better, that of an entrancing fakir, who can make flowers spring up around a chair. Sadly, such a trick is always prepared, and can only astonish once![54]

The raucous reception of *Histoires naturelles* owed much to the seeming banality of the poetry itself. More radical still was Ravel's setting of the texts, which prioritized the inflections of spoken language above the conventions of sung declamation: the songs elide or apocopate the mute 'e', the *schwa*, which is traditionally articulated when sung. Little wonder, then, that the denizens of the SNM considered *Histoires naturelles* at best incompetent and at worst deliberate mockery, another attention-seeking ploy from a five-time loser of the Prix de Rome. Never had a song premiere prompted such an extended and furious critical debate. Almost all the leading critics and intellectuals published lengthy review articles, many of them opening into wider-ranging discussions of Ravel's music, the nature of French song and contemporary musical aesthetics in general. That response demonstrates both the increasing recognition of *mélodie* as a field of serious compositional endeavour, and the now undeniable significance of the composer who, over the course of five years, had made his way to the centre of French musical conversation.[55]

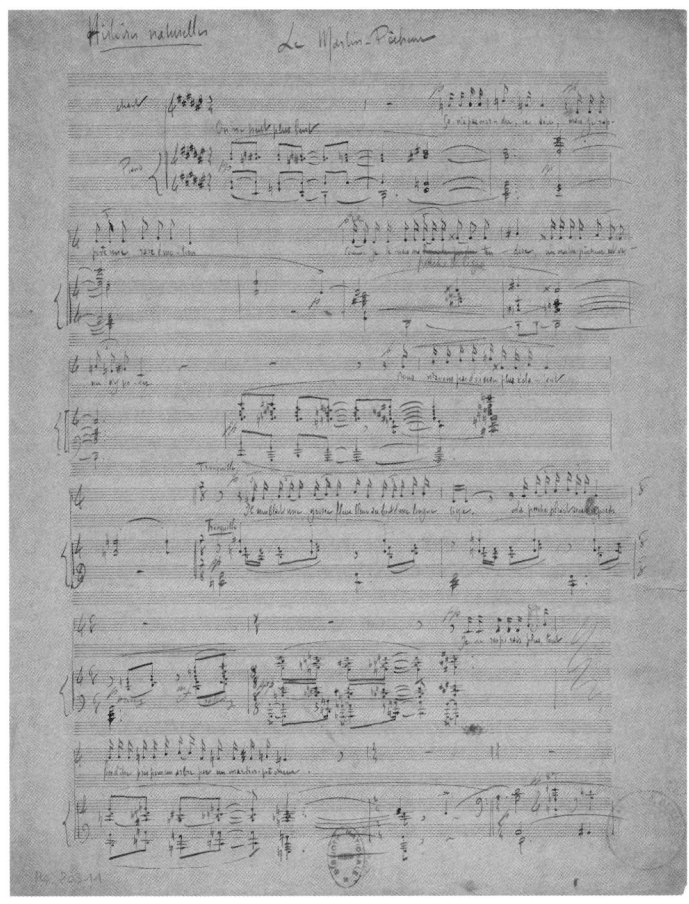

Autograph manuscript of 'Le Martin-pêcheur' (*Histoires naturelles*), showing annotations by Jane Bathori, 1906.

With his String Quartet, Ravel had asserted his competence and individuality in one of the most historically weighted of musical genres. In *Shéhérazade*, he had deliberately reclaimed a title that he had feared in 1900 would haunt him. He was sufficiently confident in the pianistic originality of *Miroirs* – premiered less than a month before Viñes gave the first performance of Debussy's first triptych of piano *Images* – to challenge one of the most powerful of the Parisian critics in their defence. And with *Histoires naturelles*, he had, equally purposefully, overset convention in full knowledge of the uproar it would cause. Ravel had now taken charge of the narrative, riding this latest *scandale* secure in his craft and his artistic principles.

3
Dances with History

For all his growing assurance, by the early spring of 1907 it was clear that in *Histoires naturelles* Ravel had provoked more of a reaction than he had bargained for. On 19 March Pierre Lalo devoted his regular column to an unrestrained demolition of the songs and *Une barque sur l'océan* (which Ravel had recently orchestrated), extending his charges to encompass Ravel's entire oeuvre and aesthetic. 'Facile and mediocre' young composers, Lalo wrote, had not just poached the mantle of *debussysme* but had grown so arrogant as to consider Debussy himself *passé*. Ravel responded in an open letter to *Le Temps*, in which he angrily distanced himself from the views that Lalo attributed to the 'younger generation':

> M. Lalo does not name the 'young musicians' that he accuses so lightly. However, my name being cited rather frequently in the course of the article could give rise to a regrettable confusion, and unsuspecting readers might think that it is about me [. . .] I do not care whether those who know my works only through reviews think me a shameless plagiarist. I will not, however, even by those sorts of people, be taken for an imbecile.

Lalo's reply, printed alongside Ravel's letter on 9 April, was malevolent. Without seeking the composer's permission, he reproduced the letter that Ravel had sent him after his review of *Miroirs*, its assertion that *Pour le piano* had contained 'nothing really new' shattering beyond recovery the fragile relations between Ravel and Debussy. A final fiery exchange appeared in *Le Temps* on 7 May.

Ravel demanded that Lalo limit himself to musical criticism and refrain from libellous mischief-making; Lalo in response bluntly accused Ravel of dishonesty and concluded 'the most obvious of his gifts is that of imitation.'

'I cannot tell you how touched I am by your interest in my music,' Ravel wrote to the critic and impresario Georges Jean-Aubry on 23 March. 'Recently people have been devoting a great deal of effort to proving that I'm deluded, or rather, that I'm trying to delude others. I cannot but confess sometimes to a certain frustration.'[1] That impulse perhaps worked itself out in his song *Sur l'herbe*, the composition of which exactly spans the period of the Lalo articles. Ravel's rapier wit emerges from the last line of Verlaine's sardonic poem, 'Hé! bonsoir la Lune!' ('Good evening, Moon!'). Fleetingly but unmistakeably, the piano quotes Debussy's 'Clair de lune', from the recently published *Suite bergamasque*.

But with his professional practice and integrity thus impugned, Ravel also needed a less subtle riposte, one that would place his originality and ambition beyond question. With this professional imperative was entwined a deeply personal one. In June 1906 Pierre-Joseph Ravel had suffered a mild cerebral haemorrhage, and by the summer of 1907 he was failing rapidly, 'barely able to walk'. The positive reviews, when they came, now meant more than ever, Maurice wrote, for the joy they brought his parents.[2] After a decade of institutional rebuff and critical vitriol, the surest route to recognition lay in opera: as Émile Vuillermoz would write satirically four years later, 'a single act at the Opéra-Comique is of more musical importance than three symphonies, ten quartets, twenty sonatas and a hundred songs.'[3] But although *La Cloche engloutie* had the scope Ravel sought, it wasn't progressing, and its Symbolist themes surely felt too risky, too open to cries of *debussyste* imitation. So, in the spring of 1907, Ravel set aside the five-act grand opera and took up a Spanish-themed farce by the Parisian playwright, poet and librettist Franc-Nohain.

A long-time collaborator of the *opéra-bouffe* composer Claude Terrasse, Franc-Nohain seems initially to have conceived his *L'Heure espagnole* as a potential libretto: an outline titled *L'Heure du muletier* appears in a list of projects he offered Terrasse in 1902. By 1904, however, he had realized it as a one-act play, which enjoyed a run of more than one hundred performances at the Odéon theatre. Principled, generous and progressively inclined, Franc-Nohain was happy to collaborate with a provocative young composer. In a cordial note of 16 April 1907 he granted Ravel permission to set his text, and proposed a meeting; within a month Ravel would write that he was 'working like a horse', the opera 'almost half done. But I'm spending whole days on it, just taking time for meals and going out to sniff the air a little in the evenings.' By 6 July he was able to present the director of the Opéra-Comique with a first 'audition'. '[Albert] Carré began by finding the subject a bit risqué,' he reported to Ida Godebska. 'The action begins a bit slowly etc. Tidy that up a bit. Of course I agreed, with no intention of doing anything about it. Once it's finished I'll come back and see him. I've heard from several sources that there's enough there to give me good hope.' By mid-autumn, the score complete, he was awaiting the director's final decision. But, he wrote sadly, 'Things are not well at home. My father is weakening continually [. . .] I no longer have any hope that he will see my work on stage: he is already too far gone to understand it.'[4]

The plot of *L'Heure espagnole* turns around the mercurial Concepcion, who lives for the one morning a week on which her clockmaker husband, Torquemada, goes out to wind the municipal timepieces, leaving her at liberty to entertain her suitors. On this particular Thursday her plans are upset by the arrival of the muleteer Ramiro, who brings a watch for Torquemada to fix. Concepcion has the ingenious idea of hiding her two swains, the poet Gonzalve and the banker Don Inigo, inside large clocks, and employing Ramiro to carry them up to the bedroom for her. As the 'hour' progresses, however, Concepcion becomes frustrated by Gonzalve's self-absorption and Inigo's ineptitude, while Ramiro's strength, compliance and unassuming manner become increasingly attractive; eventually, she invites the muleteer upstairs 'without a clock'.

In the preface to his play, Franc-Nohain offered a tale 'of unabashedly French humour, in arbitrarily Spanish costume'.

Alexandre Bailly, costume designs for Gonzalve, Concepcion and Inigo (*L'Heure espagnole*), 1911.

The ultimate target of both playwright and composer was, of course, not Toledo but Paris. Jean Périer (who had created the role of Pelléas in 1902) was to play Ramiro with what several critics noted was a working-class Parisian accent, while Ravel, in a pre-premiere interview, would speak of 'a Spain seen from the heights of Montmartre'.[5] Although dance rhythms and Phrygian turns flicker throughout the score, flamboyant musical *espagnolade* is constrained almost entirely to parodic contexts: Gonzalve introduces himself with a series of extravagant habaneras, and Ramiro's shaggy-dog story of the Barcelona bullring is ornamented with flamenco flourishes. Only in the final quintet does Ravel let rip, with what Richard Langham Smith describes as 'a brilliant double-parody, firstly of flamenco vocal techniques and Spanish inflections, and secondly of eighteenth and nineteenth-century operatic traditions'.[6] There is, the five characters sing, just 'un peu d'Espagne autour' – no more than 'a touch of Spain' about the whole affair.

Most of the action of *L'Heure espagnole* is conveyed through swift exchanges of dialogue, set with the speech-like naturalism Ravel had honed in *Histoires naturelles* (he would describe the songs as 'études' for the opera[7]). Musical coherence derives from the signature motives that usher the characters on and off the stage, their witty exchanges a direct translation of the dramatic action. The periodic interventions of the cuckoo clocks offer a less subtle humour, while spotlighted uses of Wagner's 'Tristan' chord likewise suggest a comic shorthand ('thwarted desire!'). This motivically driven storytelling has an obvious ancestor: in a harshly critical review of the first production, Auguste Sérieyx would declare, 'we are in the presence of a work conceived and ordered according to the traditional means magisterially enshrined by the master of Bayreuth.'[8] Sérieyx, of course, was – equally magisterially – missing the point. In *L'Heure* Ravel appropriated a technique conceived by Wagner for an epic of gods and heroes, and gleefully served it up as caricature, in the shrunken frame of a bedroom farce.

On 14 January 1908 Ravel was invited to present his opera to Carré once more. He recounted the occasion to Ida Godebska, his indignation tempered with unquenchable humour:

> I hum more off-key than ever, begin by breaking three strings on a dance-hall piano, let Bathori attack the bravura passages, and we await the supreme decision: Refused . . . It is impossible to impose such a subject on the innocent ears of the Opéra-Comique subscribers. Think of it: these lovers enclosed in clocks that are carried up to the bedroom! We know very well what they are going to do there!! [. . .] I realize now, thanks to that severe moralist, the director of the Opéra-Comique, that [. . .] the least innocent foible of Carmen, Manon, Chrysis or Queen Fiamette was picking their nose too much.[9]

But Ravel now had back-up: he had enlisted the support of Louise Cruppi, a prominent hostess and social activist, wife of a rising leftist politician, and the dedicatee of his *Noël des jouets*. 'Her first impulse was to write to Carré,' his letter continues. 'After mature consideration she decided nevertheless to follow her impulse, and the most pungent exchange of correspondence followed.' Mme Cruppi emerged triumphant: on 15 February *Le Courrier musical* announced, 'M. Carré has just accepted, for the Opéra-Comique, *L'Heure espagnole*, a one-act work by Maurice Ravel.'

On the heels of *L'Heure espagnole*, in the autumn of 1907 Ravel had composed a work in which his new friend Manuel de Falla would recognize a 'subtly genuine Spanishness'.[10] *Rapsodie espagnole* too keeps a tight hold on the reins of 'exoticism'. The opening 'Prélude à la nuit' suggests patches of vivid colour – the swirl of a skirt, a snatch of song – glimpsed through a nocturnal mist, while the 'Malagueña', opening with taut pizzicato and *pianissimo* lower strings, reserves the brass and percussion for brief, exuberant bursts. Again, it is only in the concluding 'Feria' that Ravel gives himself over to orchestral excess, the pent-up energy of the preceding movements released in spiralling figurations and explosive glissandi (soon to be echoed in the 'Danse infernale' of Stravinsky's *Firebird*).

For the third movement of *Rapsodie espagnole*, Ravel retrieved the 'Habanera' from *Sites auriculaires*. His incorporation of this early work, and the prominent addition of the date '(1895)' in the published score, was a pointed reminder that in the field of *espagnolade*, at least, he had been ahead of Debussy. On the eve of the premiere of Debussy's *Estampes* on 9 January 1904, Meg de Saint-Marceaux had recorded in her journal, 'it seems that Debussy has stolen the principal theme of a *Habanera* [Ravel] wrote ten years ago.'[11] 'Stolen' is too harsh a term – Debussy was experimenting with 'Spanish' colourations as early as his *Chanson espagnole* of 1883 – but his 'La Soirée dans Grenade' unmistakeably marks out its habanera rhythms on the same C♯ pedal that Ravel had employed in 1895. Its central *Tempo rubato* passage, moreover, rests on the same dominant seventh chord that, above the insistent pedal, forms the most characteristic harmonic scrunch of Ravel's 'Habanera'. In the wake of the *affaire Lalo*, Ravel had some justification for ensuring that there would be no confusion about whose habanera had come first.

Over the first two months of 1908, Ravel gave a series of composition lessons to the slightly older Ralph Vaughan Williams. His assignments included orchestrating passages of Borodin and Rimsky-Korsakov: 'He showed me how to orchestrate in points of colour rather than lines,' the English composer recalled.[12] That task reflects something of Ravel's own preoccupations, for he was busily orchestrating *Rapsodie espagnole* – a work whose own debts to Borodin and Rimsky have been observed by Steven Baur.[13] The premiere at the Concerts Colonne on 15 March 'went well', as Ravel reported to Jean-Aubry, relievedly noting a warm public reception: 'the critics were more tepid, but that matters less.'[14]

With one major work successfully launched and *L'Heure espagnole* now beyond his control, by the end of March Ravel was turning his attention to new projects: 'I'm going to get back to it. [To] what? *Cloche engloutie, Trio, Symphonie, St François d'Assise*? Don't know yet.' The idea of an oratorio on Ricciotto Canudo's *Saint François d'Assise* bubbled along for a time but went nowhere, and while he took up *La Cloche engloutie* again, he found it no easier to progress ('God! How it's aged! It will have to be started again'). By midsummer, hopeful of seeing *L'Heure* announced for the 1908–9 Opéra-Comique season, Ravel was correcting the proofs of the vocal score and tackling the orchestration. Meanwhile, the question he had pondered in March had been answered. On 17 July he wrote to Godebska, 'After three long months of gestation, *Gaspard de la Nuit* is about to see the light [. . .] It's been the devil in coming, *Gaspard*, which makes sense since He is the author of the poems.'[15]

'He' is Gaspard himself, a name perhaps best rendered in English as 'Old Nick'. Few texts capture the Gothic imagination so perfectly as Aloysius Bertrand's vivid prose-poems, first published posthumously in 1842. But in an age of elaborate literary flourish, *Gaspard de la Nuit* is also remarkable for the tension between its richness of imagery and what René Chalupt incisively described as a 'total absence of sentimentality', the 'fleeting, impressionistic vision of a moving world' matched by a 'gift for kindling atmosphere with neither description nor development'.[16] The spine-tingling intersections of technical virtuosity and explosive emotional effect, within rigorously delineated boundaries of expression and form, could not have been better suited to Ravel. His piano triptych paints the sulking tear of the water-sprite 'Ondine', the spider spinning its grisly necklace around the hanged man's neck in 'Le Gibet' – the octatonicism here surely a deliberate pun – and the hallucinatory spirals and curtain-tugging of the malignant dwarf 'Scarbo'. And yet beneath Ravel's wild 'caricatures of Romanticism', as Roy Howat has shown, pace the coolly rational outlines of the Classical sonata form, their quiet authority unswayed by the music's surface contortions.[17] It is the meticulous engineering of these structures that assures their emotional concentration: the lament that rises through the centre of 'Le Gibet' bears the laconic indication *sans expression*.

Bertrand's *Gaspard* is prefaced by a tale of a purported encounter, on a park bench in Dijon, with Gaspard himself, a mysterious figure who thrusts his manuscript into the hands of the incredulous poet. In a dreamlike opening dialogue, Bertrand makes clear that his prose-poetry is, in part, a response to one of the great questions of his age: what is 'inspiration', and where does it come from? 'Et le diable?' ('And the devil?'), the narrator asks. 'Il n'existe pas' ('He doesn't exist'), Gaspard responds. 'Et l'art?' 'Il existe.' In bringing to life a text from the age not just of Chopin (whose B-flat minor Sonata, with its grim 'Marche funèbre' and disconcerting, whispering finale, unquestionably echoes in 'Le Gibet' and 'Scarbo') but of Liszt, Paganini and Berlioz, Ravel wrote himself into the historiography of the virtuoso, deftly shading its affiliations with the supernatural, the mysterious and the macabre. Where, and who, is the artist-creator? *Il existe*.

Gaspard completed, in September 1908 Ravel took himself to Valvins and the Godebskis. Cipa and Ida were on holiday, so he relaxed in the role of uncle and co-conspirator to Mimi and Jean. 'Family life now resumes,' he wrote to Godebska: 'laborious conversations with Miss [the children's English governess], with the help of gestures and dictionaries, stories to tell the kids, not too scary at bedtime, to prevent nightmares, lugubrious in the morning, to stimulate the appetite.'[18] Mimi later recalled:

Ravel at home, *c.* 1910.

> Of all my parents' friends I had a predilection for Ravel because he would tell me stories that I loved. I used to climb on his knee and indefatigably he would begin, 'Once upon a time . . .' And it would be *Laideronnette* or *La Belle et la Bête* or, especially, the adventures of a poor mouse that he made up for me.[19]

During that visit in 1908, with the ink barely dry on the most virtuosic of his piano pieces, Ravel wrote his very simplest, a duet to charm the dreams of a sleeping princess. A little over a year later 'Pavane de la Belle au bois dormant' would be supplemented, at Durand's urging, by four more musical fairytales, collectively forming the suite *Ma mère l'Oye*.

Ravel the storyteller is vividly present in *Ma mère l'Oye*. The Beast of 'Les Entretiens de la Belle et de la Bête' ('Conversations of the Beauty and the Beast'), who growls and stamps within the unperturbed rhythms of the waltz, surely confirms Hélène Jourdan-Morhange's description of the composer acting out his tales, 'arching his back, his index finger raised mysteriously beside his nose, changing his looks and, like a child, believing in his metamorphosis, amusing himself by adopting a deep, cavernous voice'.[20] The end of 'Le Jardin féerique' ('The Fairy Garden') similarly evokes not just the story but the very act of storytelling. While the fanfares and shimmering glissandi are a transparent 'happy ever after', they also return us gently but inexorably to the real world: the chiming bells become the striking of the clock in the nursery, the end of the story, and time for bed.

A few weeks after Ravel had composed his 'Pavane de la Belle au bois dormant', on 13 October 1908, Pierre-Joseph Ravel died. Within weeks Marie and her sons had moved to a new apartment, at 4 avenue Carnot, and in the subsequent months they kept one another close. Organizing a meeting with Charles Koechlin in January 1909, Ravel asked his friend to come to them: 'my brother is away and I cannot leave my mother to lunch alone.' Perhaps the most telling indicator of the strength of his feelings is the letters of sympathy he would send over the next few years, particularly to those who had lost their own fathers. 'You still have your mother, and friends who love you,' he wrote to Léon-Paul Fargue in November 1909. 'All this makes the pain of living worthwhile.'[21]

Ravel's professional practice now spanned an ever-widening range of activities. In the spring of 1909 he made his first concert tour to Britain, hosted in London by Ralph and Adeline Vaughan Williams. At the Bechstein (now Wigmore) Hall, Ravel accompanied Jane Bathori in his *Cinq mélodies populaires grecques*, *Shéhérazade* and extracts from *Histoires naturelles*. After their rowdy début in Paris, the phlegmatic British reception of what *The Times* termed 'three delicious studies in natural history' perhaps surprised and doubtless amused Ravel. Meanwhile, among Fauré's less public but decidedly radical innovations as director of the Conservatoire was to invite his thrice-expelled pupil on to a series of juries; in 1913 Ravel would also be invited to compose a test piece (*Prélude*) for the piano sight-reading *concours*. His contributions were solicited for various collective compositional efforts, from a volume of settings of the poet Paul Gravollet in 1903 (the rather forgettable song *Manteau de fleurs*) to a special edition of the *Revue musicale SIM* in 1909 marking the centenary of Haydn's death (the tenderly acerbic *Menuet sur le nom d'Haydn*). His assured orchestration also drew some intriguing commissions. In January 1910 he cobbled together and reorchestrated some passages of Rimsky-Korsakov as incidental music for a performance of the play *Antar*, and in the spring of 1913 he would collaborate with Stravinsky to complete and orchestrate Musorgsky's *Khovanshchina*, following a commission from the impresario Serge Diaghilev.

Ravel's Russian sympathies also prompted him to enter the folksong competition organized in 1910 by La Maison du Lied (House of Song). This was a Moscow-based organization founded by the soprano Marie Olénine and her husband, the scholar Pierre d'Alheim, who had played a crucial role in introducing the music of Musorgsky and his compatriots to Paris around the turn of the century. The competition invited entrants to set seven traditional songs (Spanish, French, Italian, Flemish, Russian, Scots and 'Jewish' (*hébraïque*)). Ravel carried off the prizes for his Spanish, French, Italian and Yiddish settings, which were published collectively by Durand in 1925 as *Chants populaires*. (His Scots song, an attractive arrangement of 'Ye Banks and Braes' that plays on a sharpened Lydian fourth, was published in 1975; his Flemish and Russian settings are untraced.)

The period between 1909 and 1911 also saw Ravel entwining himself in a major realignment of the Parisian musical scene. Over the preceding decade the SNM, dominated by the adherents of Vincent d'Indy and his Schola Cantorum, had become mired in a fractious conservatism, and by 1909 factional ruptures were spilling into the musical press. For Ravel, the breaking point came when the committee refused several works by his students and friends. To Koechlin, who had just seen the first of his *Études antiques* rejected, Ravel wrote on 16 January 1909:

> Societies, even national ones, cannot escape the laws of evolution. However, one is free to withdraw from them. That is what I have done, by the same post, in resigning my membership. I had presented three works by my students, of which one [Delage's *Conté par la mer*] was particularly interesting. Like the others, this was refused. It did not present the sturdy qualities of incoherence and boredom, which the Schola Cantorum has baptised as structure and profundity [. . .] I'm planning on forming a new society, more independent [. . .] Would you join us?[22]

Within a year Ravel, with Koechlin and several other colleagues, had succeeded in establishing the Société musicale indépendante (SMI), its mission, as set out in the *Mercure de France* on 1 April 1910, to

> create a free environment, where all sorts of artistic experiments, with no divisions of genre, nationality, style or school, will be equally welcomed; where all the lively energies of our young generation will unite fraternally, in order that the finest performances possible are placed at the disposition of all.

The inaugural committee of the Société musicale indépendante, 1910. Ravel, standing second from left, leans over the shoulder of Fauré (at the piano).

Ravel had also pulled off a remarkable coup, enlisting Fauré – a founding member of the SNM in 1871 – to serve as the president of the SMI. In 1899 Fauré had implored Ernest Chausson to keep Ravel's *Shéhérazade* overture on a concert programme, when the committee had threatened to revoke its acceptance ('wouldn't it be too cruel to strike his name from the programme while he is occupied morning to night in copying the parts? Shouldn't our Society be encouraging younger composers?').[23] Fauré's assumption of the new society's presidency reflects that same liberal outlook, and the generous collegiality he maintained for his students.

Fauré also brought his political adroitness to bear in the musical press. On 20 April 1910 *Comœdia* published an interview signed by Louis Vuillemin, headed 'In the absence of the Director of the Conservatoire, M. Gabriel Fauré speaks to us of the SMI.' The conversation begins with Fauré refusing the gambit of a Schola–Conservatoire duel, observing mischievously, 'It is 4:25; the Director usually departs at 4pm,' and therefore 'I can only give you my personal opinion [. . .] All these tales of schisms, disciples, schools, don't they seem utterly dull?' He concludes forcefully, 'It is with real pleasure that I agreed to preside over a committee in which I have complete confidence, and in which I find not just former students but loyal friends.'

That evening, the SMI mounted its inaugural concert, the programme comprising Vaughan Williams's *On Wenlock Edge* and the premieres of Fauré's song cycle *La Chanson d'Ève*, Ravel's *Ma mère l'Oye* and Debussy's *D'un cahier d'esquisses* – the last of these performed, in another noteworthy act of diplomacy, by Ravel himself. Despite some scandal-seeking critics (Vuillemin discerned some 'whistles and guffaws', which he attributed delightedly to 'the principal militants of the Schola Cantorum'), the concert was a success, the press applauding both its artistic merit and the promise of a reinvigorated concert scene.

Ravel's decision to premiere his disarmingly simple duet suite at this inaugural concert was a decisive rejection of *scholiste* 'profundity'. So too was the inscription he scrawled on a score of *Ma mère l'Oye*: 'to Erik Satie, grand-papa of the "Entretiens" and much else, with the affectionate homage of a disciple'. Reclaiming this renegade composer as a forerunner of the avant-garde was both a frank acknowledgement of Satie's progressive impetus, and a new lineage to set against the Franckist SNM.

Nine months later, on 16 January 1911, Ravel played Satie's second *Sarabande* and third *Gymnopédie* at another SMI concert, together with his own transcription of the prelude to his 1891 incidental music for *Le Fils des étoiles*. Calvocoressi's review of that

Letter from Ravel to Fauré after the inaugural concert of the Société musicale indépendante, 21 April 1910, expressing his admiration for *La Chanson d'Ève* and his gratitude for Fauré's public support: 'today, more than ever, I am happy to be counted among [your] students and <u>friends</u>.'

concert would hail Satie as 'the most important and the most direct precursor to M. Debussy, to M. Ravel'.[24] By 1913 Viñes had premiered a series of Satie's piano works, Calvocoressi had written more glowing reviews, and a clutch of previously unpublished pieces had reached print, from the *Sarabandes* of 1887 to the newly composed *Véritables Préludes flasques (pour un chien)* and *Embryons desséchés*. In March 1911, meanwhile, Debussy organized a much-publicized concert that featured his orchestrations of Satie's first and third *Gymnopédies*, alongside music of his own.

Ravel's advocacy took less public forms, too. In the summer of 1912 he wrote to the composer and pedagogue René Lenormand, who was then compiling a treatise on contemporary harmony, pointing out that he had 'omitted the composer who should perhaps hold the most important place: Erik Satie'.[25] Lenormand duly revised his text, and his *Étude sur l'harmonie moderne* appeared in 1913 with four extracts from Satie's early works. All this prompted a serious shift in Satie's standing, his precarious career and wildly idiosyncratic output reconfigured in the character of 'the precursor'. If at first somewhat bemused, Satie was genuinely grateful to his younger colleagues (although within a few years he would turn harshly on Ravel). 'The progressive musical press is wholly for me,' he wrote to his brother in January 1911, and before Debussy's concert, in a note addressed to 'mon bon Ravel', he wrote simply, 'I owe this to you.'[26]

Some listeners suspected that Satie was also the unidentified author of a new piano piece that Louis Aubert performed at an SMI concert on 9 May 1911. That evening's programme was an intriguing experiment: works were presented anonymously, with audience members encouraged to suggest, on a slip of paper, the most likely perpetrator of each. Those plumping for Satie found themselves outnumbered, however, by the slim majority that correctly identified Ravel as the author of the suite *Valses nobles et sentimentales*.

If Ravel's elegant pairing of adjectives nods to Schubert's *Valses nobles* and *Valses sentimentales*, the work otherwise betrays little Schubertian imprint. Nevertheless, in its titular homage *Valses nobles et sentimentales* declares itself openly as a work in dialogue with the musical past. Various models flit through the seven waltzes: the shadow of Strauss hovers in the seventh, there is a whiff of Satie about the second, and concentrated echoes of Chopinesque chromaticism in the fifth. More broadly, *Valses nobles et sentimentales* is Ravel's most Schumannian cycle, its waltzes, diverse fusions and disjunctions, and recapitulatory finale evoking the spirit of *Carnaval*.[27] (Itself a collection of portraits and homages, Schumann's *Carnaval* even includes a 'Valse noble', and a tribute to Chopin.)

On the day of the premiere of his *Valses*, Ravel would have been found not superintending Aubert's rehearsal but at the Opéra-Comique: after more than three years of prevarication on the part of the theatre's director, *L'Heure espagnole* was at last on the billboards and the rehearsal stage. Ravel plainly enjoyed this long-awaited rehearsal period immensely. He was a regular presence in the theatre from the opening read-through in February to the final dress rehearsals, coaching singers, superintending orchestral sectionals and meticulously coordinating the layout and operation of his innumerable clocks, chimes and automatons.

L'Heure espagnole opened on 19 May to a predictably polarized critical reception. Pierre Lalo wrote of 'cold and formal irony' and 'pinched smiles', Camille Bellaigue of 'decadence': 'The "young masters" of our time [. . .] stand not for life, but for nothingness.'[28] While many critics found the relative lack of over-the-top *buffo* writing inexplicable, others – including some of Ravel's staunchest supporters – were concerned by the frivolity of his subject. 'One felt a degree of embarrassment in seeing such rare and musical gifts, an unmatchable artistic ingenuity and singular technique, thus expended in a pointless adventure,' wrote the usually enthusiastic Vuillermoz, while Jean Marnold described the libretto as 'a farce as banal as it is coarse'.[29] Nevertheless, Marnold praised Ravel's score warmly, labelling it 'a small masterpiece of invention, originality and verve [. . .] In musical terms, *L'Heure espagnole* is, since *Pelléas*, the most forcibly original and accomplished work that our French school has bestowed upon the lyric stage.' Ravel would doubtless have rejoiced, too, in Fauré's warm approbation: 'how many delightful pages, marvellous harmonic and orchestral discoveries and subtle ingenuities there are, how much gaiety and wit!'[30]

L'Heure received only a handful of performances before disappearing from the repertory of the Opéra-Comique, its mixed reviews and low receipts seemingly bearing out Carré's initial reservations. But the director had played Ravel a backhanded turn. By pushing the premiere so late in the season, he had effectively scuppered the opera's chances of establishing itself and put paid to the possibility of revivals. Within a decade, *L'Heure espagnole* would be staged at Covent Garden (1919), New York and Chicago (1920) and Brussels (January 1921), and make a triumphant return to the Opéra de Paris in December 1921. It would not appear again at the Opéra-Comique until 1945.

By mid-July 1911 Ravel had left for Saint-Jean-de-Luz, where he remained into the autumn, working feverishly to complete another long-anticipated project. Some two years earlier he had been approached to provide a new work for Diaghilev's Ballets Russes. 'I must tell you that I've just had a crazy week: preparation of a ballet libretto for the next Russian season,' he had written to Meg de Saint-Marceaux on 27 June 1909. 'Working until 3am almost every night. What complicates things is that [choreographer] Fokine doesn't know a word of French. I only know how to swear in Russian. Despite the interpreters, you can imagine the flavour of these discussions.'[31] If the composer's excitement and enthusiasm for his new project bubble off the page, this letter also hints at the tensions that dogged *Daphnis et Chloé* from conception to (and beyond) its premiere.

Michel Fokine had originally 'dreamed of hearing in *Daphnis* [...] the resurrected music of ancient Greece', his vision extending to the 'authenticity' of the music itself. Ravel had a very different notion in mind, at once highly specific and impossible to pin down. He was, he said in his 'Autobiographical Sketch', 'less concerned with archaicism than with a fidelity to the Greece of my dreams, one that corresponds freely with that imagined and depicted by French artists at the end of the eighteenth century'. If these differences in conception might have been reconciled, Fokine's memoirs speak to a more fundamental incompatibility of collaborative practice: 'It was essential for me to have [Ravel] feel exactly as I did at each moment,' he wrote.[32] That was an impulse to which Ravel was never going to submit. The composer felt wedged, and tempers frayed.

Nevertheless, by the end of 1909 Ravel was grappling seriously with *Daphnis et Chloé*, and by May 1910 he had finished the piano score and was tackling the orchestration. This first completed version of the score, however, shows a very different 'Danse générale' from that which was to conclude the ballet of 1912, its energetic triple metre seeming almost tame against the compulsive asymmetry of the $\frac{5}{4}$ final version. It was probably this bacchanale that claimed Ravel's attention in the summer of 1911, although it would not come easily: Aubert recalled that Ravel – perhaps only half-joking – even asked him to write the finale 'and I will sign it' (Aubert sensibly refused).[33] Only on 5 April 1912, two months before the premiere, did Ravel sign off on the orchestral score.

Daphnis et Chloé opens with the ritual adoration of Pan and the presentation of offerings by the young men and women. A competition is proposed whereby Daphnis and the cowherd Dorcon will dance for the reward of Chloé's kiss. Dorcon's 'Danse grotesque' is met with a resounding burst of orchestral guffaws, but Daphnis wins the palm and takes his kiss. A band of pirates burst on to the stage and abduct Chloé; Daphnis, rushing in just too late, finds only her sandal, and casts himself down before the nymphs' grotto. As he sleeps, the nymphs dance and summon Pan. The second scene takes place in the pirates' camp, where, amid the brass-dominated revelry of the 'Danse guerrière', Chloé pleads for freedom and attempts to escape, her futile struggles accompanied by a circular octatonic melody in the piccolo. Pan intercedes and the pirates flee before a host of satyrs. The transition to the final scene is effected through the dazzling 'Dawn' music. Daphnis wakes to find Chloé restored to him, and the ballet concludes in joyous celebrations, including a re-enactment of Pan's love for the nymph Syrinx.

A lot thus happens in three scenes, although, as Roger Nichols notes, the main events are mostly conveyed through tightly compressed musical episodes. The pirates' irruption on to the stage, pursuit and seizure of Chloé, for instance, occupy less than a minute, the actual abduction accomplished within the space of four bars.[34] Juxtaposed with those concentrated intervals are Ravel's most luxuriant musical soundscapes, the 'Dawn' scene and no less glorious 'Introduction', in which the bass A^1 – a fundamental in every sense – unfolds with fifth upon fifth into a sweeping universe of sound. There, surely, was Ravel's idiosyncratic nod to Fokine's idealized music of the ancients.

Two more ballets claimed Ravel's attention over the winter of 1911–12. Between Christmas and New Year he drafted a scenario for *Ma mère l'Oye* at the request of Jacques Rouché (director of the Théâtre des Arts). This 'Sleeping Beauty' narrative involved weaving a new Prelude from fragments of the existing suite movements, adding a 'Danse du rouet' to depict the spindle and the pricking of Princess Florine's finger, and orchestrating the whole. The reordered inner movements of the original suite figure as tales to charm the princess's dreams, before at the end of 'Laideronnette' hunting horns are heard, and another 'dawn scene' (with bird calls and falling fourths echoing in miniature the apotheosis of *Daphnis*) ushers on Prince Charming, who awakens the princess to the celebratory harps and bells of 'Le Jardin féerique'. Despite its hectic pace – the ballet opened on 29 January, just a month after Ravel's first conversation with Rouché – this enterprise was an entirely happy one. 'I didn't dare hope for the total joy, so delightful to a composer, of seeing a work for the theatre realized exactly as he had conceived it,' Ravel wrote gratefully.[35]

He then turned immediately to orchestrating and grafting a scenario onto *Valses nobles et sentimentales*, at the behest of the dancer and director Natalia Trouhanova. This collaboration, now titled *Adélaïde, ou, le langage des fleurs*, was more fraught. Two days before the 22 April premiere, the harassed composer arrived to conduct what he thought was to be a working rehearsal, only to discover that it was the *répétition générale* (the open dress rehearsal). Worse still, the ballet wasn't yet up to scratch. 'This won't do at all,' he wrote to Trouhanova. 'Arm yourself with patience: you are going to see just how tedious I can be during a rehearsal.' He signed off, though, with a touch of humour: 'I would have liked to have sent some flowers with this *pneumatique*. But given its tone, perhaps a bunch of nettles would have been more appropriate.'[36]

By the end of the month *Daphnis* too was in rehearsal, the friction between its creators only amplified by the intensity of the rehearsal process. Jacques Durand recalled 'loud discussions' among the Russians (Fokine, designer Léon Bakst, principal dancer Vaslav Nijinsky and Diaghilev); Fokine, who handed in his notice midway through rehearsals, would later describe *Daphnis* as 'the most sorrowful work of my entire life'.[37] The tension was compounded by the *succès de scandale* of the other new ballet in the company's season, Nijinsky's audacious rendering of Debussy's *Prélude à l'après-midi d'un faune*. Diaghilev inserted extra performances of Debussy's ballet at the expense of Ravel's, dispensing with the *répétition générale* and delaying the premiere by three days. Only two performances of an under-rehearsed *Daphnis*, therefore, were given

Léon Bakst, costume design for *Daphnis et Chloé*, 1912.

before the Ballets Russes' season ended on 10 June. Years later, Ravel admitted to Misia Sert that 'poor *Daphnis* has plenty of grounds for complaining about Diaghilev. I know it was not all on one side and that few productions have ever caused such trouble, but it wasn't always the work's fault.'[38]

And yet, in a marker of the transformation Diaghilev's Ballets Russes had already wrought on the Parisian musical scene, it was

Ravel's *symphonie chorégraphique*, even more than his one-act opera, that cemented his standing. 'After *Daphnis et Chloé*', wrote Vuillermoz,

> it will become difficult to compare Ravel's technique to the meticulous labours of tiny sailors, patiently rigging up a three-masted ship in the depths of a bottle; the spontaneity of his harmonic language, the freshness of his new ideas, the textures of his orchestra [. . .] all point to an artistry that is securely and definitively mastered.[39]

Although *Daphnis* inevitably divided the critics, those who remained implacably opposed to all Ravel represented were beginning to find themselves rather isolated.

After another three-month sojourn in Saint-Jean-de-Luz, the last months of 1912 passed in correcting the orchestral proofs of *Daphnis* (all 308 pages of them, Ravel groaned to Raoul Bardac).[40] He was also corresponding regularly with Stravinsky, and on 10 November he was present at a memorable private preview of *The Rite of Spring*, given by the composer for the Apaches at Delage's Auteuil studio. 'You must hear Stravinsky's *Rite of Spring*,' Ravel would write presciently to Lucien Garban on 28 March 1913. 'I believe it will be as important an event as the 1re [premiere] of *Pelléas*.' A month later he was helping to arrange Stravinsky's accommodation for the epoch-making premiere: suggesting a hotel neighbouring his own apartment on avenue Carnot, he wrote cheerfully to Stravinsky, 'That way we'll be able to exchange "courtesies" from our balconies in our pyjamas.'[41]

In November 1912 Stravinsky had told Ravel about a radical new song cycle by Arnold Schoenberg that he'd heard on a recent visit to Berlin: 'a *melodeclamation*, *Pierrot lunaire* [. . .] I have never heard anything like this in music.'[42] By January 1913 the committee of the SMI had resolved to programme *Pierrot lunaire*, which they hoped to mount alongside Stravinsky's brand-new *Three Japanese Lyrics*. Two months later Ravel, holed up with Stravinsky and *Khovanshchina* in Clarens, was 'bitten' in turn by the *Japanese Lyrics*.[43] On 2 April he wrote to the SMI committee to outline a 'stupendous proposal for a scandalous concert'. The first two items on the programme – the Schoenberg and Stravinsky cycles – would 'make the audience howl', he wrote, but the last 'would send them out whistling tunes': '2 poésies de S. Mallarmé: Maurice Ravel'.[44] By the autumn of 1913 two poems had become three, and the 'concert scandaleux' took place on 14 January 1914, Ravel's *Trois poèmes de Stéphane Mallarmé* programmed alongside the *Japanese Lyrics* and Maurice Delage's *Trois poèmes hindous*. (*Pierrot lunaire*, whose conception and ensemble had offered a prompt for all three composers, was not heard in Paris until 1922.)

Although Ravel's Mallarmé *Poèmes* represent some of his most abstruse harmonic language, they bear little resemblance to either Schoenberg or Stravinsky. Instead, every musical element – form, timbre, texture, harmony, pitch – is brought to bear on the chiselled symbolism of Mallarmé's words. The third of his chosen poems, 'Surgi de la croupe et du bond' ('Risen from the crupper and the leap'), depicts the ornate form of an empty vase, which holds neither water nor the flower towards which it aspires. The rigid poise of the vase is traced through the formal contours of the sonnet, its promise evoked through the imagery of meeting lips and the final evocation of the rose, an ancient symbol of fulfilment and perfection. The 'still-life' quality of the poem perhaps prompted Ravel's luminescent play of instrumental colour: alone of the three songs, 'Surgi de la croupe . . .' employs bass clarinet and piccolo, and relegates the strings to muted tremolandi, harmonics and sustained chords.

More intriguingly, the symmetrical outlines of Mallarmé's vase also find equivalence in Ravel's manipulation of form and line. The architectural mirroring of the modified ternary form is reinforced by the very appearance of the score, in which the upward arabesques and sinuous melodic lines of the outer sections vividly suggest the leaping form of the vase. The corresponding blankness of the staves of the central passage, in which piano chimes resonate in near-silence, is both visually and aurally evocative of its empty belly. Ravel's tonal plan equally suggests an element of visual thinking: the song is underpinned by the tritone opposition C/F♯, representing an exact division of the octave, and respectively the 'emptiest' and 'fullest' key signatures. In the final bar, the piano returns to the bass C as the voice sings the key word 'rose' on $f^{1}\sharp$. For the space of one quaver beat we hear the tritone – emptiness and plenitude – unadorned.[45]

As the SMI was preparing for the 'Concert scandaleux', Parisian *littérateurs* were perusing the newly published third collection of Paul Reboux and Charles Müller's series of *À la manière de . . .* literary pastiches. Ravel doubtless appreciated the Mallarmé spoof that featured in that volume (of which his own copy remains in his library at Montfort-l'Amaury). In the autumn of 1913 he had been indulging in the same fashionable pastime, concocting a pair of *À la manière de . . .* pieces for piano, as part of a collaboration with his friend Alfredo Casella. Casella's first *À la manière de . . .* series, published in 1911, had opened with the inevitable Wagnerian 'Einleitung', proceeding via Brahms and Strauss ('Sinfonia molestica') to Fauré and Debussy. Ravel contributed two pieces to Casella's second collection, whose other targets include d'Indy and Ravel himself. His *À la manière de Borodine* is a sinuous waltz that unfurls from the textures and lilting harmonies of the 'Sérénade' and appended 'Scherzo' from Borodin's *Petite Suite*, with passing echoes of the String Quartet no. 2 and the Polovtsian dances from *Prince Igor*. *À la manière d'Emmanuel Chabrier* is more sophisticated still: in a brilliant, multilayered portrait of not just Chabrier's idiom but his era, Ravel reworked the 'Jewel Song' from Gounod's *Faust* to incorporate a plethora of fleeting quotations and 'Chabriesque' fingerprints. The closing bars bring *four* composers into dialogue. Reprising the ascending stepwise gesture that ends Chabrier's 'Sous bois' (*Pièces pittoresques*), Ravel sails close to the very end of *Tristan und Isolde*, the opera that transformed Chabrier's musical language.[46] Ravel thus sketches a portrait of Chabrier as he might have improvised on Gounod's warhorse aria in the salons of the 1860s, the Wagnerian twist thrown in for those with an ear to catch it.

Between 1912 and 1914 Ravel also made his only serious venture into musical criticism, penning a dozen reviews for the

Revue musicale SIM and *Comœdia illustré*.⁴⁷ He cultivated a lively, provocative manner, sometimes rivalling Debussy's mouthpiece Monsieur Croche in cheekiness. *Parsifal*, he concluded, was 'less entertaining than *La Vie parisienne*. All the same, it is less boring than the *Missa solemnis*, that inferior work by Beethoven.'⁴⁸ (His lifelong anti-Beethovenian stance was doubtless a reaction to the cultish reverence then accorded particularly to the symphonies and late quartets, but also for what he saw as a certain coarseness of orchestration, in particular.)

Ravel's observations on actual performances are often perfunctory, overshadowed by his sprightly perambulations through musical history and tradition, and a notable readiness to marry principle and practice. He called out César Franck for certain faulty orchestral doublings, with the acute observation that 'Just when the inspiration is at its peak, one is disconcerted by extraneous sonorities'; and he put his finger on the tension between the freshness of inspiration and the weight of self-conscious tradition in Brahms's symphonies, praising his orchestration but lamenting his 'learned, grandiloquent, convoluted and heavy' developments. A performance of *Les Idéals* prompted an extended musing on Liszt's diffuse legacies: notwithstanding his 'truly prodigious musical generosity', Ravel concluded, Liszt's shortcomings were the source of Wagner's 'overly pompous vehemence', of 'the heaviness of [Franck's] elevation', the occasional 'gaudiness' of the Russians and the extreme 'coquettishness' of the French.⁴⁹

Ravel also took aim at the reactionary bent of musical criticism – hardly surprising in the light of his own experience – and he was a notably vehement defender of Debussy ('the most important and profoundly musical composer living today'). A piece on Debussy's orchestral *Images* opens with the declaration, 'The objective of the official representatives [of musical criticism] has always been [. . .] to weaken the younger generation, whose tendencies appear dangerous to them'; it ends by upbraiding critics for 'gradually closing their eyes before the rising sun, while loudly proclaiming that night is falling'.⁵⁰

But Ravel's most strident language was reserved for Wagner – or rather, for *wagnérisme*. Of d'Indy's *Fervaal*, he observed, 'this "music drama" is Wagnerian in the very essence of its music, in its theatrical organization, in its philosophy, the realization of that philosophy, the symbolic function of the characters and their allusive language.' While he admitted that a work entirely devoid of analogies with its predecessors could be nothing but a 'monstrous exception[,] one feels a certain discomfort in recognizing [those analogies] in such great numbers, all coming from the same source, and reunited in the same work.'[51] A review of Camille Erlanger's *La Sorcière*, published a fortnight earlier, makes a similar argument. In both articles Ravel drew attention to defective prosody, underlining the essential incompatibility of the French language with Germanic musical procedures. Of the 'turbulent declamation' of *La Sorcière*, he noted, 'The comprehensibility of the text, which is so vital in the theatre, cannot help but suffer.'[52] Like his strictures on Brahms and Franck, Ravel's aesthetic charge – that it was no longer acceptable for French composers to be writing in a Wagnerian manner – was thus grounded in a sharply practical critique.

Throughout the first decade of his career, it had been friends such as Vuillermoz and Calvocoressi who had essentially spoken for Ravel, defending and explicating his aesthetic to a sceptical press and public. Now, it was from a place of some security that he could afford to take to the progressive musical press, not just to launch entertaining critical rockets but to advance a philosophy of his own. Sending his article on Debussy's *Images* to the journal's editor, Ravel wrote, 'This is, I think, not at all what you asked for. It's more combative – but I believe it's what had to be said.'[53]

4
An Unknown Destination

'An elevating excitement of the soul – quite independent of that passion which is the intoxication of the Heart – or of that truth which is the satisfaction of the Reason.' This was the epigraph, drawn from Edgar Allan Poe's essay 'The Poetic Principle', that Roland-Manuel chose to head the first biography of Ravel, published early in 1914. One of a series commissioned by the publisher Durand to honour its leading composers, *Maurice Ravel et son œuvre* would sit alongside essays on Debussy, Fauré, Saint-Saëns and d'Indy. What the latter two composers made of this elevation is unrecorded – although while Roland-Manuel was hard at work, Saint-Saëns was expostulating to a colleague that *Pavane pour une Infante défunte* typified the deplorable present condition of French music ('the very title is an absurdity').[1]

Most of Roland-Manuel's forty-page text is devoted to a survey of Ravel's music and its critical reception, including an uncompromising account of the short-sightedness of the Institut and Conservatoire, and a few potshots at Pierre Lalo. More interesting is the concluding reflection on Ravel's aesthetic, his influences and the vexed question of 'originality'. Challenging the old saw of *debussysme*, Roland-Manuel sought to establish an alternative compositional lineage through Chopin, Liszt, Chabrier, Satie and the 'Mighty Handful', highlighting characteristic distinctions between Ravel's and Debussy's harmonic languages. He then tackled the assertion, already deeply ingrained in the critical record, that beneath its glittering surfaces Ravel's music was emotionally barren. Weaving the thread of his epigraph with

Ravel at the piano with Vaslav Nijinsky in the Ravel family apartment at 4 avenue Carnot, February 1914. Photograph by Alfredo Casella.

strands drawn from Ravel's own musical criticism, he argued that the composer's detractors had mistaken an absence of 'pseudo-profundity' for a lack of feeling altogether, for they recognized emotional intensity only in a Wagnerian grandiloquence that was 'entirely removed from the French spirit'. In claiming for Ravel Poe's 'poetic principle', Roland-Manuel asserted that his teacher had 'miraculously' recovered the 'lost thread of our purest tradition [...] which once belonged to Couperin and Rameau'.[2] It is thus through a distinctly literary framework that this first biography binds Ravel firmly into the historical tapestry of French musical endeavour.

Ravel himself, meanwhile, had 'taken refuge' in Saint-Jean-de-Luz. 'I've various things to finish,' he wrote on 1 February 1914, 'and it's become impossible in Paris.'[3] He was contemplating a piano concerto on Basque themes titled *Zazpiak-Bat* ('the seven are one', referring to the seven provinces of the Basque region), *La Cloche engloutie* was still limping along, and the 'grand waltz' *Wien* (Vienna) was back on his agenda after an eight-year absence. He had also been commissioned by the Russian soprano Alvina Alvi to arrange two traditional Jewish melodies, the secular 'L'Énigme éternelle' (from the Yiddish folksong 'Die alte Kasche') and the sacred 'Kaddisch'.

But Ravel's first job, on his arrival in the Basque country, was to transcribe a *forlane* by Couperin, the last movement of the fourth *Concert royal* (1722). This little project was prompted partly by the sort of spoof that he adored, not least for its anti-clerical streak. Pope Pius x had recently banned Catholics from dancing the 'lascivious' tango, proposing the *forlana* as an acceptable alternative. In response, the April 1914 issue of *La Revue musicale SIM* featured a light-hearted historical survey of the *forlana* by the journal's editor, Jules d'Écorcheville. The seriousness of that essay can be deduced from the final musical example, which rewrites Wagner's 'Ride of the Valkyries' in the manner of an eighteenth-century *forlane*.

Ravel probably undertook his transcription at Écorcheville's prompting: a cheeky note to Cipa Godebski, explaining that he intended to have it danced at the Vatican by Colette and Mistinguett in drag, is very much in the spirit of the enterprise.[4] However, he seemingly failed to produce the copy in time for press, for the issue appeared with a more sedate rendering of Couperin's *forlane*, by Albert Bertelin. It would be neither the first nor the last occasion that Ravel, failing to meet a deadline, nevertheless found himself hooked. The transcription that he did belatedly realize, with its hand-crossing in the third *couplet* and grace-note octave chimes in the fourth, demonstrates that his creative attention was well and truly engaged.[5]

If Couperin's *forlane* had set some compositional wheels spinning, Ravel's delay in completing it was doubtless the result of a project, first contemplated six years earlier, that was rapidly claiming his entire attention: a monumental Piano Trio. Although it resurfaced in his correspondence only on 19 March 1914, the Trio must have been percolating well before his departure from Paris, for by the 23rd of that month he had signed off the expansive first movement. April and May vanished with engagements in Geneva, Lyon and Paris, but by the last week of June Ravel was hard at work

Ravel, photographed by Roland-Manuel on the banks of the Nivelle, Saint-Jean-de-Luz, 1914. Behind him is the village of Ciboure; he was born in the tall house in the middle of the picture (now 27 quai Maurice Ravel).

back in Saint-Jean-de-Luz, enjoying the 'beautiful sky, the heat and the flies of my homeland'.[6] There is no mention there, nor in any of his surviving letters over the next month, of the gathering storm.

When it came, on 3 August 1914, the declaration of war seemed to stun Ravel utterly. 'I cannot go on: the nightmare of every minute is too terrible. I think I'll go mad,' he wrote to Godebski. His mental turbulence reveals itself in his ellipses, sudden shifts of mood and uncharacteristic hyperbole. He was in a terrible quandary: 'No! I've no right . . . but nor do the others, and yet . . .' he agonized to Godebski, and the next day, to Maurice Delage:

> to leave my poor old mother would surely be to kill her. And after all the fatherland isn't waiting for me to save it . . . But hour by hour, I can feel that reasoning cracking . . . and so as not to hear it, I'm working. Yes, I'm working, and with a mad certainty and clarity. But at the same time the blues are at work too, and I suddenly find myself weeping over my flats! Naturally, when I go down and appear before my poor mother, I must appear calm, if not light-hearted . . . will I be able to keep this up?[7]

By 8 August, however, Ravel was writing firmly to his brother, 'I've taken the wisest course: I'm going to join up.'[8] Édouard had come to the same resolution, and within weeks would be serving as an ambulance driver and stretcher-bearer. By the time his family saw him again, over a year later, his hair had turned white.

His decision made, Ravel's capacity to work returned. The second half of August was spent in a frantic effort not just to finish the Trio but to prepare the score for a publication process that might have to proceed without his oversight: he was, he wrote, considering it 'an *œuvre posthume*'. In early September, buoyed by professional relief and nationalistic fervour, he travelled to Bayonne to enlist – and was confounded to find himself rejected for active service. 'They wanted none of me,' he wrote to Durand; 'I'm 2 kilograms too light to be a soldier.' Instead, he passed the early autumn in Saint-Jean-de-Luz, caring for the wounded, writing roll calls of his scattered friends, and considering his next compositional move. The sketches for *Zazpiak-Bat* had been left in Paris, and two projects he'd long been contemplating were now politically untouchable. *La Cloche engloutie* – derived from a German play – 'really is [sunk] this time', and as for *Wien*: '!!!', he wrote simply to his friend Hélène Kahn-Casella, 'no way I can rename it *Petrograd*.'[9]

Instead, Ravel confided to Roland-Manuel, he was planning a 'French suite' for piano: 'no, it's not what you think, the Marseillaise is nowhere to be found, there will be a forlane, a gigue, no tango though.' He had, it seemed, returned to Couperin's *forlane*, and found in it the seeds of *Le Tombeau de Couperin* (that title was soon settled, appearing in his correspondence from January 1915). But for the first time in two decades, composition was not enough:

> for God's sake, for God's sake, I know perfectly well, my dear friend, that I'm working for the fatherland by writing music! At least, so I've been told enough times in the last 2 months to convince me, first to try to stop me joining up, and then to console me for being rejected. It didn't stop me, and I'm not consoled.[10]

By 10 November Ravel had returned to Paris with a new plan: following his brother's example, he was going to enlist as a driver. In between driving lessons, he busied himself trying out his Trio with Alfredo Casella (piano), George Enescu (violin) and Joseph Salmon (cello). The oft-remarked discrepancies between Ravel's manuscript and the first edition of 1915 are plainly the result of rehearsal experience, the musicianship of these exceptional performers helping the composer to rework several passages in which the original figurations and dispositions teeter over the edge of the possible.[11]

Ravel's revisions particularly affect the 'Pantoum', a scherzo of extraordinary technical and compositional virtuosity. His title acknowledges a poetic form originating in Malaysia (*pantun*) and popularized in France by Baudelaire, whose best-known *pantoum* is 'Harmonie du soir' (set by Debussy in 1889). The *pantoum* requires the second and fourth lines of one strophe to become the first and third of the next, each line heard first as a consequent becoming the antecedent to a new consequent in turn. In his *Petit Traité de poésie française* (1872), Théodore de Banville explained that this sophisticated patterning engenders a distinctive dual form:

The Enescu Trio – George Enescu (violin), Alfredo Casella (piano) and Louis Fournier (cello) – in 1904. With the cellist Joseph Salmon, Enescu and Casella would workshop Ravel's Trio with the composer in the autumn of 1914.

'from beginning to end [. . .] *two themes* are pursued in parallel.'[12] Brian Newbould has shown how precisely this premise – the alternate development of two themes that 'may be extricated and reassembled as separate, intelligible entities' – maps over the skittering quavers of Ravel's 'Pantoum'.[13]

To the autograph score of his Trio, Ravel appended a four-page analytical sketch that sets out the work's themes and compositional principles. His analysis concludes with a single, curious line: 'You will observe that the various subjects that figure in the four movements of the Trio are all independent.' The briefest examination, however, reveals that the first three movements start with the same melodic cell, a three-note gesture of dominant-subdominant-dominant (that is, a step down then up again). The joyous 'Final' inverts that, moving instead one step *up* and down again; the melody of bar 1 also features the same pitches as bar 3 of the solemn Passacaille, in reverse order. Ravel's denial of cyclic procedures was doubtless a jab at the laboured aesthetics of the *scholiste* faction. His assertion nevertheless compels us to consider what happens beneath the musical surface: if the motivic congruence is obvious, the compositional craft lies in the entirely different directions in which the material can be driven. As Poe wrote of 'The Raven', 'I determined to produce continuously novel effects by the variation of the application of the refrain, the refrain itself remaining, for the most part, unvaried.' Each time we wheel around to meet the same material it lands differently, its structural import changed by its new position in the dance.

In his memoirs, Jacques Durand described a rehearsal of Ravel's Trio at Salmon's home, in which he and the performers found themselves wholly 'carried away'. It was, he wrote, an hour 'marked with a white stone in my memory', in which all present were able briefly to forget 'what was going on "over there"'.[14] Such moments of oblivion were desperately rare. A few days after his return to Paris, Ravel had been shattered to receive word that his Basque 'cousins' Pierre and Pascal Gaudin had been killed, side by side in their trench, on their first day at the front. 'My poor Marie [. . .] What can we say to you, my God!' wrote Ravel to their sister. 'That they died gloriously . . . that may be true for them, but for you, for your parents, what a shocking horror! Mama is devastated. She repeats over and over: "poor children!"'[15]

It was perhaps in response to the deaths of the Gaudin brothers that in the last weeks of 1914 Ravel composed 'Trois beaux oiseaux de paradis', a setting of his own poetry for unaccompanied mixed choir. Shot through with the melancholy refrain 'Mon ami z-il est à la guerre' ('My love is at the war'), the song invokes the colours of the French flag: the three birds bear in turn an 'azure-coloured gaze', a kiss placed upon 'a snow-white brow', and 'a beautiful crimson heart'. 'Ah, I feel my own heart growing cold/ Bear it with you also,' the solo soprano sings, as the wordless accompanying voices fade to an empty unison.

At the beginning of 1915 Ravel added two more songs (and poems) to complete his *Trois chansons pour chœur mixte sans accompagnement*. 'Nicolette' is a distorted Red Riding Hood, whose titular heroine escapes the wolf and rejects a beautiful page before leaping into the arms of a fat, ugly and fabulously wealthy lord, the folklike minor modality finally subverted with an ironic *tierce de Picardie*. 'Ronde' speaks first in the voices of the 'old women' and 'old men', who warn the young boys and girls not to go to the woods of Ormonde, which are filled with all manner of fantastic creatures ('Hamadryades, dryades, naïades, ménades, thyades, folettes,/ Lémures, gnomides, succubes, gorgones, gobelines . . .'). The final verse, again, has a sting in its tail. The young people sing that they will not go to the woods, for the creatures are no longer there: 'The foolish old men and women have frightened them away.' The harmonic clarity and abruptly sparse textures belie the outward exuberance of the perfect cadence: harsh reality stamps furiously upon the fairytale.[16]

Each of the *Trois chansons* is inscribed to someone whom Ravel hoped would expedite his enlistment. 'Nicolette' was offered to Tristan Klingsor, who had connections with senior military officials; 'Ronde' to Sophie Clemenceau, a salon hostess, family friend and sister-in-law of the politician Georges Clemenceau. Paul Painlevé, the dedicatee of 'Trois beaux oiseaux du paradis', was a cabinet minister and a specialist in aeronautics – he would become war minister in 1917 before briefly assuming the premiership – whom Ravel had met in the Clemenceau salon.

This third dedication betrays Ravel's new ambition: to join the flying corps. On 10 March 1915 he was declared fit for auxiliary military service, and immediately enlisted; within a week he had been assigned to the 13th Artillery Regiment as a truck mechanic, servicing vehicles at a Parisian depot. But, as he wrote to the music critic Edwin Evans, he was only there 'while I wait to become an aircraft bomber, which, for the last 8 months, has been my sole preoccupation'. His younger brother was unimpressed. 'Now that you're in the truck service you'd do better to stay there than to try for the planes,' he advised. The damn things kept crashing – and 'you should see the state of the poor blighters I'm bringing in every day.'[17]

The year 1915 passed slowly, for there seemed little prospect of Ravel being sent to the front, let alone transferred to the Air Force. Some diversion came in the form of editing the piano music of Felix Mendelssohn: with German editions both unobtainable and undesirable, Durand had enlisted several leading composers to re-edit canonic repertoire. (Debussy tackled Chopin and Fauré Schumann, while Saint-Saëns produced several volumes of Mozart.) Compositionally, however, the year was a blank. Ravel had finished the *Trois chansons* by February and saw the Trio through the press, but there is no hint of him even contemplating anything new. 'I'm sure I'll be able to work [at the front],' he wrote hopefully to Roland-Manuel in mid-December.[18]

By the new year of 1916 Édouard was home, and Maurice was at last on the verge of departure 'for an unknown destination'. More delays intervened, but on 10 March he was dispatched to 'X, not very far from the front'. 'X' was Bar-le-Duc, a crucial staging point at the head of the sole route that remained open to Verdun, some 50 kilometres (30 mi.) to the north. 'Although we're well away from [the front] it feels very close,' Ravel wrote to his mother a week after his arrival. 'Everything reminds you of it. Planes are going that way, and convoys full of soldiers. At every junction there's the same indication: V. . . and an arrow.'[19] Although he promised Marie that he was in no danger, within days Ravel was driving into Verdun itself to retrieve vehicles, fuel and supplies. To Ida Godebska he wrote, on 2 April, an account of such a mission worth quoting at length. After a 4 a.m. departure and a white-knuckle journey along a road so damaged that Ravel feared his truck would overturn, they arrived at the gates of the ancient fortress town:

> We shake ourselves: stiff and sore muscles, but nothing's broken [. . .] The remains of a great street: all the houses torn apart – or in heaps of stones. In a little square, a bizarre display: wardrobes, an old bench, a piano, some cooking utensils. A little further, by some fragments of a wall, an elegant Directory teapot, silver salt-cellars on a Gothic trunk – the remains of an antiques shop [. . .] All this is pathetic, but the horror of it still hasn't grabbed you. But here: we are at the centre of the town, the river. On one side, the terraces of the old city, dominated by the cathedral. Along the quay, picturesque houses, the theatre, the grand boatmen's café. On the other bank, magnificent buildings, newer hotels, almost all of it seemingly intact. The sun is shining; not a cloud in the sky.
> . . . and suddenly anguish seizes you. You have just realized: in this great nightmare town, there is nobody, absolutely nobody. The silence is hallucinatory, yes, the silence. The duel of the artillery nevertheless continues; almost regular, like a thunderous game of tennis. Up there, explosions, whistles, the rattle of carriages, those little balloons of white smoke coalescing and aligning. But all of that is somewhere else; it glides above this appalling silence.[20]

Two days later he recounted the same experience to Jean Marnold. 'I will doubtless see more horrifying, more repugnant sights,' he concluded; 'I do not think I will ever experience anything as profound and strange as this sort of mute terror.'[21]

By mid-April Ravel had been moved to Monthairons, just 15 kilometres (9 mi.) south of Verdun. 'Before going to bed,' he wrote, 'we watch the fireworks. Sometimes we see them a little too well. And all night we are lulled by the cannonade.' 'Of course,' he added, in this letter to Godebska, 'don't tell Mama that I'm in any danger.' 'Don't tell Mama' had become something of a refrain. To his wartime 'godmother', Mme Fernand Dreyfus (mother of Roland-Manuel), he wrote that he had 'brought [Mama] up to date with my present circumstances; I've even told her that we're relatively close to the battle – that way, she'll see that I'm concealing nothing – but I haven't told her about the dangers I could be running.' By the end of April these included crashing his truck (twice), running several more missions into Verdun, driving through falling shells, and returning to a site he'd visited that morning to find a bomb crater in its place. In early May he spent five days ('and nearly as many nights') searching for damaged cannon, driving without lights 'along impossible roads, rocky or boggy, filled with ruts and craters, obliged to pass in the midst of shells exploding to right and left, behind and in front', with a load twice as heavy as his truck should have borne: 'Needless to say, Mama doesn't know about all this.'[22]

'All this' proved too much for Ravel's truck, a Panhard he had christened 'Adélaïde', which broke down completely on 6 May, leaving him to play Robinson Crusoe (as he put it) in the woods for more than a week. Once rescued, he was deposited at Chamouilley, some 20 kilometres (12 mi.) south of Bar-le-Duc, to await repairs in a lodging of unexpected beauty. His glassless window overlooked waterfalls, woods and trailing roses, the noise of the water and abundant birdsong muting even the distant cannon. Billeted with a family of evacuees, he diverted himself making paper hens and breadcrumb ducks for the children.

But life at Chamouilley quickly became interminable. Not only did Adélaïde continue to 'rot in the corner of the depot' ('someone comes along now and again and removes a small part'), but Ravel's own health was also increasingly fragile. Making one final attempt to be transferred 'to the planes', he presented himself for a medical inspection in late May, only to be informed that he was suffering from mild hypertrophic cardiomyopathy (thickening of the muscular walls of the heart). 'Oh! Not much, and it's not serious,

In uniform, 1916.

they tell me,' he wrote to Marnold, but it had definitively put an end to his dreams of aviation. He couldn't bring himself to appeal to a more senior medic, for he was 'scared stiff' of being transferred out of active service altogether and sent back to a desk job. And, of course, 'I've not said anything to Mama.'[23]

'Don't tell Mama' was one thing, 'Don't tell Maurice' quite another. Marie Ravel's health had been failing for at least eighteen months, and when Ravel learned through Marnold that she was suffering from repeated nosebleeds, he was horrified. Édouard was a frustratingly poor correspondent, his intermittent and telegraphic missives only fuelling his elder brother's agitation, and Marie herself was not writing to him at all. 'You know you don't have to write literature,' Ravel begged his mother. 'Give me your news, tell me what you're up to, the visits you've received, what's happening with Édouard.' By the end of June his hectoring had compelled Marie to begin writing 'daily', although the renewed correspondence brought its own concerns: 'Dearest Mama, you mustn't have insomnia! Have you told the doctor? [. . .] You know a lack of sleep is the worst thing for your health.'[24]

As in the early months of the war, Ravel found his lack of agency crippling. 'The life I'm leading here is so stupid, utterly useless,' he complained to Marie Gaudin; in other letters he too began to complain of the insomnia that would shadow him for the rest of his life. Moreover, he wrote to Marnold on 7 June, 'For the last few days I've been suffering from something else. I suddenly realized that I could no longer live without music [. . .] For almost two years I thought I had forgotten it, and it's returned like a searing pain.' And to Mme Dreyfus he confided a month later, 'Truly I've never been so much a musician, I'm overflowing with inspiration, with projects, with all sorts of chamber music, symphonies, ballets.'[25]

If composing was beyond his reach, Ravel nevertheless kept up with the mechanics of his professional life, corresponding with Lucien Garban about rights and royalties, corrections for reprints and a potential four-hand arrangement of the Trio. He also found himself unable to escape the capital's charged musical politics. In early June he received a letter from the critic Charles Tenroc, inviting him to sign up to the 'Ligue nationale pour la défense de la musique française', a new organization dedicated to the suppression of contemporary Austro-German music. Ravel unhesitatingly refused. Addressing the Ligue's statutes point by point, he firmly refuted their assertion that music had an 'economic and social [function]: I have never considered music or the other arts in that light.' Moreover, he argued, 'It would be dangerous for French composers to remain deliberately ignorant of the work of their foreign colleagues and to turn into a sort of national clique: our musical art, which is presently so rich, would soon degenerate, enclosing itself in commonplace formulae.'[26] In response, Tenroc warned Ravel that his championship of France's 'enemies' might lead to his own music being 'sacrificed' – and, indeed, no works by Ravel were programmed in the series of 'Festivals de musique française' that the Ligue mounted between June 1916 and June 1917.

Over the summer of 1916 a second front opened in the clash of societies, in the form of a push to re-amalgamate the SMI with the SNM. Led by the pianist Alfred Cortot, then *chef de service* for musical propaganda, this was dubbed the *union sacrée* in echo of the truce that bound opposing political parties for the duration of hostilities. Ravel did initially agree to join this endeavour, encouraged by the nomination of Fauré as a consensus president. Over the course of the autumn, however, it became increasingly clear that the SNM was seeking to subsume and suppress the progressive SMI. By November the leading figures of the younger society were united around the position that a reunified organization under the single banner of the SNM was to be resisted. Fauré made some efforts to bring the parties together, but satisfied nobody. Émile Vuillermoz wrote dispiritedly to Charles Koechlin that their old *maître* had 'disappointed but not surprised them, because his real sympathies lie with the *salonniers* – Bréville, Lalo, etc.'[27] In Fauré's defence, he was then in his seventies, leading the wartime Conservatoire through the busiest administrative period of the academic year, and desperately anxious about his son Philippe, who had spent most of 1916 at Verdun and by November was hospitalized in Nice; he had no appetite for factional rows. In the end, a contentious gathering on 17 December saw the proposed amalgamation soundly rejected. The *union sacrée* disintegrated into recriminations, litigated across a series of bitter polemics in *Le Courrier musical* through the spring of 1917.[28]

Meanwhile, after a short and welcome leave in early August 1916 Ravel had returned to Chamouilley and immediately contracted dysentery. Sent to the garrison town of Châlons-sur-Marne (now

Châlons-en-Champagne) to recuperate, by mid-September he had additionally been diagnosed with a hernia and admitted to hospital, where he underwent an operation on 30 September. When he returned to Paris to convalesce, he found his mother seriously unwell and deteriorating rapidly. Marie died on 5 January 1917, with both her sons at her side. She was buried two days later in a civil ceremony: indomitable Marie, who had once declared 'that she would prefer to be in hell with her family, rather than in heaven all alone', would have no priest at her ending.[29] The mourners included Fauré, Diaghilev, Satie, Misia Edwards and Marguerite de Saint-Marceaux, who wrote caustically: 'The two brothers were in utter despair [. . .] They couldn't stand upright. Both were in pieces, incapable of response or self-control. Lamentable spectacle at this time where heroism comes as naturally as breathing.'[30]

The death of his mother was the great watershed of Ravel's emotional life, and the blow for which, despite all his anxious letters and his devoted attendance in her final weeks, he was utterly unprepared. Roland-Manuel wrote that Ravel's friends found him sunk in a kind of 'mute stupor' that no diversion could breach, helpless and inconsolable.[31] The pain of bereavement resonates through his correspondence for years: 'There will always be something broken,' he would write to Hélène Kahn-Casella in January 1919.[32] Marie's passing marked the final disintegration of the securities on which Ravel relied so profoundly, the routines and rhythms of home and work and family. Only after 1921, with the move to Montfort-l'Amaury, would he regain solid ground.

Ravel saw no more military action. While he was dispatched back to Châlons-sur-Marne on 24 January 1917, he went no further east. Physically depleted and in an emotional abyss, he was plainly unfit for service. In late March he was transferred back to the Paris depots, and on 1 June he was granted a temporary discharge on the grounds of a marked loss of weight and a suspect right lung. He never drove a vehicle again, haunted for the rest of his life by the visceral terror of his nocturnal expeditions in 1916.[33]

Ravel retreated to the home of Mme Dreyfus in the Normandy village of Lyons-la-Forêt, perhaps finding comfort in the company of a friend who was in deep mourning herself (her son Jean had been killed in action in 1916). There, some 100 kilometres (60 mi.) from the nearest point of the Western Front, he found himself able to work again. By early July he had completed the 'Menuet' and 'Rigaudon' of *Le Tombeau de Couperin*, which he dedicated respectively to the memory of Jean Dreyfus, and of Pierre and Pascal Gaudin. The other four movements followed over the course of the next few months, each inscribed to a friend *mort pour la France*. The suite was published in the spring of 1918, the funerary urn that adorns the cover designed by the composer himself.

Le Tombeau de Couperin lies squarely in the classical tradition of the literary or musical *tombeau*, an apotheosis of artistry and craft that has no need of lugubriousness. (It has a model in François Couperin's own *tombeaux*, the luminous and lively *Apothéoses* in honour of Lully and Corelli.) The pianist Marguerite Long would vigorously counter those who condemned Ravel for writing dances for the dead: 'When a musician of genius offers the very best of himself [. . .] is that not the most moving tribute?'[34] Long's husband, the musicologist Joseph de Marliave, had been killed in 1914; Ravel's 'Toccata' is dedicated to his memory.

Ravel would later describe his suite as a homage not so much to Couperin himself as to the musical spirit of his epoch, an ethos evoked in the clarity and intricacy of his textures, his meticulous ornamentation, and the symbioses of rhythm and gesture that generate the characteristic 'affect' of each movement. Beyond his original inspiration in Couperin's 'Forlane', various specific models have been posited for individual movements: Louis-Claude Daquin's popular 'Le Coucou' relative to Ravel's 'Toccata'; the 'Rigaudon' and 'Premier Tambourin' from Rameau's *Troisième Concert* against Ravel's 'Rigaudon'; and, in more general terms, the blend of simplicity and sophisticated tenderness in Couperin's 'L'Arlequine' (23e Ordre), a movement Ravel apparently adored.[35] But as Barbara Kelly acutely observes of Ravel's 'Forlane', while his *couplets* brush past Couperin's, it is the *rondeau* that demonstrates the composer's

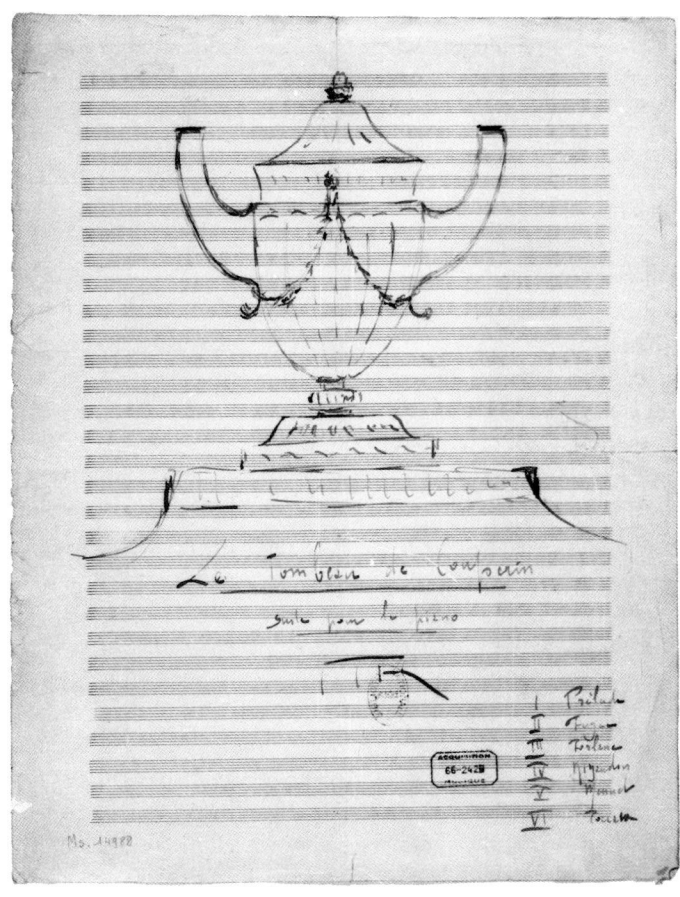

Autograph sketch for the title page of *Le Tombeau de Couperin*, 1917.

'ultimate control of his model'. With its opening leap through a characteristic major seventh, it is this spine of the movement that lies furthest from his source.[36]

The last winter of the First World War found Ravel back in the capital. The apartment on avenue Carnot was given up, Ravel and Édouard lodging instead with the family's business partners, the Bonnets, in the western suburb of Saint-Cloud. But with bombs soon falling on Paris itself, the desperate spring offensive and then the onset of the influenza epidemic, life in the city felt perilous and uncertain: unsurprisingly, 1918 was another barren year. At some point Ravel orchestrated 'Alborada del gracioso', but his only new work was the tiny and curious *Frontispice*, published as a preface to a poem by Ricciotto Canudo (the librettist of Ravel's long-abandoned *Saint François d'Assise*). The unusual scoring for piano *five* hands, as well as the polyrhythms and cumulative textures, suggest that *Frontispice* was initially conceived for pianola, probably on a commission from the Aeolian Company in London.[37]

By September 1918 Ravel's health was markedly worse. He was so exhausted, he wrote, that 'When I go to put on my underwear, I rest a little while calculating the effort that procedure demands.' He cancelled a British concert tour and a planned retreat to Saint-Jean-de-Luz, and by early November was moving only between 'bed and sofa'.[38] He spent the morning of the Armistice being driven (by Édouard) to the Hôpital Lariboisière, by the Gare du Nord. There, he was diagnosed with tubercular granulomas and prescribed a protracted period of convalescence in the mountains.

Passing the first winter of peacetime at Megève, in the shadow of Mont Blanc, Ravel rested and planned. He was thinking again of *Wien* (now renamed *La Valse*) and contemplating a 'Duo' for violin and cello. In late February he wrote energetically to Colette about the libretto she had sent for a projected opera-ballet titled *Divertissement pour ma fille* (Divertissement for my Daughter), which he intended to take up as soon as he returned to Paris. 'I'm taking notes, without writing any,' he reported hopefully.[39] But back in Paris he continued not writing notes – at least, not new ones. The city's musical life was suddenly flourishing, and he found himself dashing between Conservatoire examining, rehearsals and concerts, including a much-delayed premiere of *Le Tombeau de Couperin*, given by Long on 11 April 1919. He also squeezed in some serious orchestrating. By late May he had completed not just the four movements that comprise the orchestral suite *Le Tombeau de Couperin*, but also, at the request of Serge Diaghilev, Chabrier's *Menuet pompeux*, for a ballet titled *Les Jardins d'Aranjuez* (the composite score of which also included *Alborada del gracioso* and Fauré's *Pavane*).

As the autumn passed *La Valse* was again on Ravel's mind, but he was still unable to commit notes to paper: Saint-Cloud was too close to Paris, he complained, and there was too much going on. At the beginning of December, therefore, he left for the hamlet of Lapras, in the Ardèche region west of Valence. While he hoped to repeat the restorative mountain cure of the previous winter, most of all he needed to work, and his friend André-Ferdinand Hérold (the translator of *La Cloche engloutie*) had offered his country retreat. In Lapras, Ravel found a solitude unlike anything he had previously experienced. Although he had initially feared it, he was soon revelling in his isolation, rising early to work, hiking up the mountains in the afternoon, then returning with the fading light to tackle his correspondence. At long last, his muse had returned. 'I'm working, in a way that I've not been able to for five years,' he wrote on 15 December. His relief is palpable. Wit and humour flood back into his letters ('This has got to work: not being able to travel to Vienna, I've installed myself close to . . . Vals!'), and even his mechanical metaphors function again: to Roland-Manuel he exulted, 'I've got [*La Valse*] started up at last, and I'm in 4th gear.' Although the Christmas and New Year period, around the anniversary of his mother's death, plunged him briefly into darkness, on New Year's Eve he was determinedly beginning the orchestration. By late February he was ready to dispatch the piano score to Durand, writing blithely, 'Let's hope it doesn't get lost, I haven't kept a draft.'[40]

La Valse begins at the limits of audibility, threads of half-remembered tunes drifting above a murmuring bass. The harmonic mists resolve gradually into a clear tonic/dominant pulse (fig. 9) before the main thematic material arrives at fig. 17. A suite of shorter episodes follows, building towards the first climax, then melting into the reprise. The more concentrated second orchestral 'wave' sees the waltzes briefly recapitulated, jostling each other in compressed and fragmented form before a pulsing dominant pedal sweeps them out of the way to prepare the ultimate climax. In a device borrowed directly from Chabrier's incandescent 'Fête polonaise' (*Le Roi malgré lui*), the pedal launches a long chromatic ascent from the dominant A. But while Chabrier's ascent ends at the bass F♯, Ravel's continues, across a change of key signature that marks a very audible 'handover'. As the inexorable bass mounts in five complete passes through the octave, chromatic and metric displacements and collisions spiral into terrifying chaos. While Ravel marks a firm *Sans ralentir* over the concluding bars, the conductor Manuel Rosenthal (Ravel's pupil and friend) stressed that there can be no speeding up, either: '<u>Et</u> <u>voi-là</u> <u>c'est</u> <u>tout</u>', Rosenthal chanted against the final, shattering five-note unison.[41]

Reviewing the orchestral premiere of *La Valse*, in December 1920, the critic of *Le Temps* heard the stubborn echoes of waltzes past, swirling amid the ruins of empire. Raymond Schwab, in *Le Ménestrel*, invoked the mid-nineteenth-century French climate of decadence and revolution: '"We are dancing upon a volcano" [. . .] there is an element of menace in this joyful bacchanal.'[42] We may equally read, as more recent scholars have done, a deliberate collision of pre- and post-war aesthetics, or the brutal shattering of a dream-world.[43] Yet Ravel was insistent in his rejection of extramusical narratives for *La Valse*. His scenario is carefully minimalist, a mere scene-setting that carries us barely a fifth of the way through the score:

> Through swirling mists, waltzing couples can be faintly distinguished. The clouds gradually dissipate [fig. 9], and a great ballroom is revealed, filled with a whirling throng. The stage gradually lightens. The light of the chandeliers bursts forth with the *fortissimo* [fig. 17]. An imperial court, circa 1855.

In one 1922 interview Ravel concerned himself more with explaining what *La Valse* was *not* about: 'It doesn't have anything to do with the present situation in Vienna [. . .] I did not envision a dance of death, or a struggle between life and death.'[44] A contemporaneous letter to the composer Maurice Emmanuel similarly stressed, 'All that should be understood is what is expressed in the music itself.'[45] But even Ravel later admitted (to the choreographer Sonia Korty in 1926) that '*La Valse* must be considered as a kind of tragedy.'[46] Indeed, it is difficult not to hear in those cataclysmic final bars the

Spiralling doodles on the last page of the autograph piano score of *La Valse*, 1920.

thunderclap of 1914 and the brutal severing of post-war 'Wien' from its imperial past. Whatever ending Ravel might have foreseen when he first contemplated a tribute to 'the great Strauss' in 1906, it was surely not this one.

Even as he threw himself into orchestrating *La Valse* – 'you'd better believe that I'm rising, not with the sun, but well before it' –

Ravel was nonplussed to receive a batch of papers from the
Ministry of Fine Arts, informing him that he had been nominated
for the Legion of Honour. 'I refuse,' he telegraphed instantly
to Roland-Manuel, and to Robert Brussel (a leading critic with
ministerial connections) he wrote, 'I care nothing whatsoever
for this honour, [but] I care still less for the publicity of a refusal.
What to do?'[47] Unfortunately, he was too late to do anything;
slow postal deliveries to the winter-bound Rhône-Alpes had
perhaps been compounded by his own lack of enthusiasm (as
Roger Nichols notes) for opening an official-looking envelope
while he was 'waltzing furiously'.[48] Before Ravel could convey his
refusal privately, on 15 January the nomination was confirmed by
ministerial decree, and on the 17th it was published in the *Journal
officiel*. 'Hurry up and congratulate me,' he wrote to Godebska;
'you'll never have another chance.'[49]

    Just as he had rejected the assertion of the Ligue nationale that
art served an 'economic and social function', so was Ravel firm in his
Baudelairean conviction (expressed by the poet in *Mon cœur mis à
nu* (My Heart Stripped Bare) of 1864) that artistic worth was not in
the gift of the state, and decorations conferred distinction only upon
those who lacked it.[50] The publication of the nomination before
he had accepted it – a clear and unfortunate piece of ministerial
overreach – only hardened his determination. While he might have
quietly slipped the celebrated red ribbon into his pocket (as Brussel
suggested, and Roland-Manuel later reflected), to Ravel such a
course felt intellectually dishonest. His artistic independence had
been supercharged by the rejections and disdain emanating from
the very institutions that now sought to honour him. To accept the
Legion of Honour was an impossible yielding.

    Worst of all, the whole business was a disruption. 'I spent all day
receiving telegrams,' he complained on 17 January, 'and now I'll have
to go to [the nearby town] Lamastre tomorrow to see the papers
and send a dispatch to the Ministry. What a ridiculous mess!'
Perhaps it could be put about that the *Journal officiel* had made
an error, he suggested, only half-joking – 'for Maurice Ravel, read
Maurice Rostand'? Or perhaps, if he just didn't fill in the forms and

didn't turn up for the ceremony, the whole thing might be quietly dropped?[51]

French bureaucracy being what it was, however, the withdrawal of the nomination necessitated another official decree, which was duly published on 4 April. A deluge of press attention ensued, the most famous and cutting response coming from the pen of an increasingly vituperative Erik Satie: 'Ravel refuses the Legion of Honour but all his music accepts it.'[52] 'How they're howling at me!' Ravel wrote to Georgette Marnold (daughter of the critic Jean Marnold).[53] He fled gratefully from one retreat to another, leaving Lapras in late April for the country home of his close friends Pierre and Jeanne Haour in Saint-Sauveur (Eure-et-Loire). While he warned Garban not to let anyone but the Dreyfus family know he was passing through Paris, his transit must have included a memorable meeting with Diaghilev, for whose Ballets Russes *La Valse* was now intended.

Given the fraught history of *Daphnis et Chloé*, this renewed collaboration with Diaghilev was perhaps surprising. As though the 1912 season had not been turbulent enough, in the summer of 1914 the impresario had sparked a furious row by mounting a Drury Lane production without the chorus, a cost-cutting measure the composer considered a 'mutilation', and which had prompted a strongly worded letter to the London dailies. Nevertheless, Diaghilev and Ravel had remained in contact via Misia Sert. (Having divorced Alfred Edwards in 1909, in 1920 Misia married the artist Josep Maria Sert, her long-term companion and one of Diaghilev's collaborators.) Within a week of Marie Ravel's funeral, they had met to discuss a prospective ballet titled *Le Zoo*, on a scenario by the Futurist poet Francesco Cangiullo. Although nothing came of it, the renewed communications perhaps prompted the change of conception of *La Valse*: in 1914 it appears in Ravel's correspondence as a 'symphonic poem', but by February 1919 it had become a 'poème chorégraphique', and by the time he arrived in Lapras he was certainly working with the Ballets Russes in mind.

What had remained unchanged, however, was Ravel's determination to dedicate *La Valse* to Misia. As early as July 1906 he had written to her of his plans for '*Vienne*, which is destined for you'.[54] In January 1920 it was Misia whom Ravel asked to set up a meeting with Diaghilev: 'I don't know if Serge is in Paris, and, as you know, he doesn't answer my letters.'[55] And it was *chez* Misia that Ravel and Marcelle Meyer would play *La Valse* for Diaghilev, in the presence of Stravinsky, the choreographer Léonide Massine and a 21-year-old Francis Poulenc, who left a famous account of the occasion:

> I saw [Diaghilev] was embarrassed, I saw he didn't like it and was going to say 'No'. When Ravel had got to the end, Diaghilev said something which I think is very true. He said, 'Ravel, it's a masterpiece . . . but it's not a ballet. It's the portrait of a ballet . . . It's the painting of a ballet.' [. . .] Ravel proceeded to give me a lesson in modesty which has lasted me all my life: he picked up his music quite quietly and, without worrying about what we all thought of it, calmly left the room.[56]

Camille Chevillard would conduct the orchestral premiere of *La Valse* at the Concerts Lamoureux on 12 December 1920. An unequivocal success with a pan-European press and public, it quickly confirmed Ravel's growing international reputation. But not until 1926 was it staged as a ballet (by Korty, in Antwerp), and only in May 1929 would Ravel mount the podium at the Opéra to conduct the French balletic premiere, in a staging by Ida Rubinstein.

The very first performance of *La Valse*, however, aptly took place in Vienna. With Alfredo Casella, Ravel performed his two-piano version at Arnold Schoenberg's Society for Private Musical Performances on 23 October 1920. The three-hour concert juxtaposed piano and chamber music by Ravel, Schoenberg, Berg and Webern; *La Valse*, Berg reported to Schoenberg, was added at the last minute as a gesture of goodwill.[57] Ravel professed himself delighted by the music of the Second Viennese School, and made sure to take scores home with him, declaring his intention to have them heard in Paris. Berg's op. 5 Pieces for Clarinet and Piano, performed at that epic concert, would indeed be given at the SMI in June 1921.

Berta Zuckerkandl (sister of Sophie Clemenceau), who had masterminded the trip, would recall that in accepting her invitation to Vienna Ravel declared, 'I've been waiting for the opportunity to counter this senseless hatred the war has left behind.'[58] An interview in the *Neue Freie Presse* likewise stressed the 'sympathy' Ravel claimed the French felt for the Viennese. In triumphant echo of his response to the Ligue nationale in 1917, the article closed by quoting Ravel's declaration that 'the natural calling [of music] is to be international and to bind all nations with the bond of harmony. May music also infuse the spirit of reconciliation into every heart.'[59]

5
The Compositional Machine

The year 1920 brought two sad and significant passings. Ravel's uncle Édouard died in February, and his close friend Pierre Haour in September: the last of his parents' generation, and the first of the Apaches. Yet in retracing the paths of grief, Ravel seemed to find a tentative way out of the darkness that had shadowed him since his mother's death. With *La Valse* he had finally managed to restart the compositional turbines, and in the late summer, even as he sat by Haour's bedside – for he spent several months helping to nurse his friend – he found himself oddly productive. 'We're living in perpetual anguish,' he wrote to Roland-Manuel between night watches in late August, but he was planning 'this machine for the Opéra' (Colette's opera-ballet), completing the first movement of his Duo for Violin and Cello, and sketching out the three movements that would follow.[1]

Crucially, the winter Ravel had spent in Lapras had brought another realization: he needed a home of his own, away from Paris. The loss of his uncle, although deeply felt – 'I loved him dearly,' he wrote – made that unexpectedly possible. Aided by a legacy from the painter's estate, in early spring Ravel was able to 'put out enquiries' for 'a house at least 30 kilometres from Paris'. By the end of the year he was searching in earnest, and by late February 1921 he was 'camping out' in his new home, 'chivvying along the masons, painters, carpenters, etc.'[2]

The village of Montfort-l'Amaury lies some 40 kilometres (25 mi.) west of Paris, in the department of Yvelines. On a steep, curving street between the ruined towers of a fifteenth-century castle and the cavernous parish church of St Pierre, Ravel found Le Belvédère. The house has the aspect of a sailing ship, long and narrow (though Manuel Rosenthal would describe it as more akin to a badly cut slice of Camembert[3]). In 1921 it comprised just four rooms; over the next few years Ravel would enlarge it to ten.

The visitor awkwardly negotiating the narrow passageway of Le Belvédère, its slanting steps and odd angles, is vividly aware of Ravel's birdlike stature. There is a tiny, densely stocked library, a minute 'Japanese salon' and a shadowy blue music room, dominated by the 1909 Érard piano. Ravel's bedroom, on the floor below street level, is reached by a twisting stair from the kitchen and opens directly on to the Japanese-style garden. With its back turned unprepossessingly to the street, Le Belvédère looks instead towards the gentle hills of the Île de France. Ravel, who added a wide, wistaria-hung balcony above his garden, relished that view. He perhaps sensed in its contrasts a natural echo of his creative vision, ornate and concentrated interiors illuminated by the sweeping contours of the landscape.

Ravel was well aware that having removed himself from the capital, his friends and colleagues would have to come to him. He lavished time and attention on his home, designing wallpaper and hand-stencilling Grecian figures on to the dining-room chairs – or at least one of them: the joy of it, he confided to a friend, was in settling on the motif; the execution was less exciting. And he collected obsessively, filling the rooms with a panoply of trinkets, tiny games, mechanisms and figurines. Genuine antiques and exotic trifles were soon jostling with others that were prized precisely for being neither 'authentic' nor 'antique'. Of his beloved 'faux Monticello' Hélène Jourdan-Morhange once teased him, 'Ravel, it's disgraceful of you to hang that horror on the wall!' 'But I know it's fake and it amuses me,' he responded indignantly.[4]

Guests to Le Belvédère would be ritually welcomed with tours of the garden and extravagant cocktails, concocted from a special cupboard halfway down the winding kitchen stairs. (These, Jourdan-Morhange recalled, often took an inordinate amount of time to produce, the composer 'heedless of the fact that his poor visitor – often come from Paris to show him some music – might have preferred his presence to the cocktail!'[5]) In 1925 they would be entertained by the antics of a puppy Ravel christened Jazz, and from 1926, after Jazz's sadly early demise, by a pair of Siamese cats, whose peculiar conversations their owner delighted in imitating. But pets, garden, cocktails and tours existed, in 1921, only in Ravel's imagination: for the moment he did not even have central heating or a reliable housekeeper. His first employee lasted only a few months before 'ditching me', as he wrote to Roland-Manuel. 'She hadn't been gone five minutes before I learned that she was a regular in all the bars of Montfort, a fact that explained the periods of nervosity from which my crockery periodically suffered.'[6]

In place of the errant Mme Prohaska – who had absconded with his favourite umbrella, much to his distress – Ravel hired Marie-Thérèse Reveleau, who would remain with him until his death. Although friends recalled lively arguments between the irascible composer and his equally hot-tempered housekeeper, there was also much good-natured teasing and a genuine regard, which increasingly turned to quiet affection: in the hours before he slipped into a coma in December 1937, it was Mme Reveleau whom Ravel asked to see. Despite the years of renovations, the pile of radiators in the garden and the brackish water ('You'll see I'm not hiding the attractions!'[7]), in Le Belvédère Ravel at last regained his stable centre.

Although the First World War had long constrained Ravel's growing international reputation, celebrity now seemed to arrive in a rush. With the death of Debussy in 1918, followed in 1921 by Saint-Saëns, then Fauré (1924) and Satie (1925), Ravel soon found himself hailed as France's greatest living composer. In 1923 his old Conservatoire classmate Dumitru Kiriac would write to marvel affectionately at the place he now held in the international musical imagination, 'from Budapest to London and Bucharest to Vienna, in America and perhaps even in Japan. Here in Romania you are the idol of musical youth. We value and admire you.'[8]

Furnished at last with a reliable postal address, Ravel was now inundated with requests for autographs and interviews, petitions

Ravel and 'Mouni', Le Belvédère, late 1920s.

and questionnaires. 'Who are your favourite composers?' began one such document, from the British musicologist Wilfrid Dunwell:

> What do you think of Bach, of Couperin and Beethoven? To what extent is your work influenced by Spain? Do French writers and musicians often mingle? Do you yourself often discuss the principles and objectives of art with your friends? Can you explain the harmonic basis of 'L'Énigme éternelle'? What do the titles 'Malagueña', 'Habanera', 'Feria' mean?[9]

. . . and so on, and so on. Packages of scores piled up, too, sent by hopeful young composers – some of whom also presented themselves on his doorstep. Within four months of his arrival Ravel was, he lamented, being besieged by a young British composer, Ethel Leginska (born Liggins), who had 'installed' herself at Montfort in the hope that he would teach her. 'I've promised to look at a symphonic poem in the hope that I'll be able to get rid of her,' he wrote. 'Such is calm!'[10]

When his sympathy or interest was engaged, though, Ravel could be generous with both time and resources. In the immediate post-war years he gave the Russian composer Nikolai Obukhov free composition lessons while organizing a fund to support him and his family. The Polish-born Alexandre Tansman, newly arrived in Paris and entirely unknown, likewise found Ravel a willing colleague and advocate, whose introductions opened many doors to the city's musical establishment.[11] When Alfred Françaix sent some compositions by his ten-year-old son Jean, Ravel took them seriously: 'The most fertile [gift he] can possess as an artist is that of curiosity,' he wrote, gently cautioning that

> too rigorous study at an early age would stifle that [. . .] While one can't overlook technique, harmony, counterpoint, fugue, the mechanics of composition, the detailed analysis of works, all that can be really practised only when his musicality is fully developed. First, the most important thing is for him to understand music *instinctively*.[12]

To his adult pupils, however, Ravel could be a harsh master: Rosenthal recalled him furiously ripping up an attempt at a fugue and throwing the scraps into the fireplace.[13] In May 1922 he wrote unsparingly to Maurice Delage, a close friend and occasional pupil of almost twenty years:

> First, I like [the piano piece *Schumann*] very much, it's completely successful. But that's not the problem. You mustn't do that any more. Too long to explain here a bunch of things that you must have realized better than I. Nevertheless, you need to extract yourself from this impasse. If I managed it, it's not – as you might think – thanks to my natural gifts [. . .] Do you want to work? There's still time.[14]

There are echoes here of Ravel's pre-war appraisals of d'Indy and Erlanger: what is done is done well, but the path is ill chosen. 'Massenet, who was so gifted, squandered his talents through an excess of sincerity,' he wrote in similar vein in 1931. 'He truly wrote everything that came into his head, the result being that he always repeated the same thing.'[15]

By the summer of 1921 Ravel had managed to wrangle himself a functional workspace and was trying to get back to his *boulot* (his job), turning first to the Duo for Violin and Cello that he had now rechristened a Sonata. On his mind since early 1919, the first movement had served as his contribution to a special 'Tombeau de Debussy' issue of *La Revue musicale* in December 1920. By mid-March 1922 Ravel was at last able to deliver the manuscript of all four movements to his publisher. 'It doesn't seem like much, this machine for two instruments,' he wrote to Michel-Dmitri Calvocoressi, 'but there's a year and a half of slog in it. Marius – I mean Darius – Milhaud, in that time, would have produced 4 symphonies, 5 quartets and several lyric settings of Paul Claudel.'[16]

The first movement of the Sonata for Violin and Cello is a taut sonata form, the second subject of which – in curious echo of the much earlier String Quartet – is recapitulated at the same sounding pitch, the tonal contrast coming from the shifting of the harmonic

On the beach at Saint-Jean-de-Luz, *c.* 1921.

ground beneath it. The last movement, for all its tonal freedom and technical exuberance, is nevertheless grounded in a Mozartian rondo structure, including a rigorous *fugato* with a chromatically descending subject that uses ten of the twelve available pitches.

In his 'Autobiographical Sketch', Ravel would observe that the Sonata marked a 'turning point' in his career: '*Dépouillement* is pushed to an extreme; harmonic charm is renounced, in favour of an increasingly pronounced tendency towards melody.' The wording (as dictated to Roland-Manuel) succinctly acknowledges one of the primary tropes of the 1920s – the *style dépouillé*, or 'stripped-down style' – and the decade's energetic jostling for control of the aesthetic narrative. As early as February 1919 Ravel had found himself consigned by the avant-garde critic Paul Landormy to 'part of our past'.[17] In a subsequent series of articles titled 'Le Déclin de l'impressionisme', Landormy repurposed Jean Cocteau's era-defining *Le Coq et l'arlequin* (1918) to assert that the *debussyste* style was already outmoded by contrast with the 'very sober, very stripped-down [*dépouillé*] art' of the group newly baptized Les Six.[18] 'At a time when theories of the *style dépouillé* take hold of the avant-garde's journalistic columns,' Roland-Manuel had retorted in an article for *La Revue musicale* in April 1921, 'it is important to note that it is Ravel who has given us the most eloquent illustrations of this aesthetic to date.'[19]

While Ravel himself generally kept clear of such polemics, his own battles with critics and institutions had instilled a firm conviction of the rights of younger generations to make their voices heard, and indeed to react against even his own example. In newspaper interviews he offered praise and encouragement for Les Six and their peers, and in 1927 he gave a lengthy statement to Roland-Manuel defending Milhaud, Arthur Honegger and Marcel Delannoy against the attacks of Pierre Lalo (whose targets, he noted, had moved with the times). In 1923 he quietly insisted on Milhaud's inclusion on the committee of the French delegation to the International Society for Contemporary Music, despite 'an anti-Ravelian lecture' he had given in America.[20] And at the premiere of Georges Auric's ballet *Les Matelots* (1925), Ravel moved quickly to offer enthusiastic congratulations, protesting to a surprised Jourdan-Morhange, 'Why should I not congratulate him? [. . .] I like his ballet. He slams Ravel? Well, he's right: if he didn't attack Ravel, he'd be writing Ravel, and we've got enough Ravel.'[21]

Ravel did allow himself the occasional potshot at his younger colleagues. His cheeky reflection on how much Milhaud could have produced in the time it had taken him to write the Sonata for Violin and Cello (which doubtless owes something to Milhaud's recent biting dismissal of *La Valse* as 'Saint-Saëns for the Ballets

Russes'[22]) was echoed in a Danish interview, published in May 1924, in which he reflected that 'the young write too much and do not work enough.'[23] Later that year, struggling to finish *L'Enfant et les sortilèges*, he would joke ruefully, 'If only I'd been named Darius!'[24] Milhaud would later reflect that Ravel 'was very generous and always spoke of my work very nicely and it was almost a little embarrassing for me because I couldn't give him back this nice appreciation'.[25] But Ravel probably didn't mind too much. A few days after the premiere of his Sonata, given by Jourdan-Morhange and Maurice Maréchal at the SMI on 6 April 1922, he wrote to Cipa Godebski:

> I heard that my Sonata for Violin and Cello didn't please you, and that you were courageous enough to say so. That made me very happy, because it proves – not that I ever doubted it – that it was through neither friendship nor snobbery that you've liked my other works.[26]

Two days after that premiere Ravel was present at another memorable concert, organized by Henry Prunières (the editor of *La Revue musicale*), at which he turned pages for Béla Bartók as he accompanied the Hungarian violinist Jelly d'Arányi in his Violin Sonata no. 1. Milhaud was following the score at Bartók's shoulder, while Poulenc turned for d'Arányi; the guests at the subsequent soirée included Stravinsky, Karol Szymanowski, Honegger, Albert Roussel, André Caplet and the soprano Marya Freund. Ravel would meet d'Arányi again a few weeks later, when, with the cellist Hans Kindler, she gave the London premiere of his Sonata for Violin and Cello on 7 July – and spent another evening playing traditional Hungarian music for the insatiable composer.

The main purpose of this cross-Channel expedition, however, was to make a series of piano rolls for the Aeolian Company. Ravel travelled to London with Robert and Gaby Casadesus, and while he recorded his 'Oiseaux tristes' and a *Pavane* of unfussy elegance, it was Robert who made the rolls of 'Le Gibet' and the Toccata from *Le Tombeau de Couperin* (although these too were issued under

Ravel's name).²⁷ Together with *Valses nobles et sentimentales* and the first two movements of the *Sonatine*, recorded for Welte-Mignon in summer 1912, and a 1928 Duo-Art roll of 'La Vallée des cloches', these rolls constitute Ravel's only recorded performances as pianist.

In July 1922 Ravel retreated to the home of Mme Dreyfus in Lyons-la-Forêt, chased from Montfort (he wrote to Marguerite Long) by a bout of depression, the ongoing renovations and the awareness of an imminent deadline. Six months earlier the Russian conductor Serge Koussevitzky had commissioned him to orchestrate Musorgsky's *Pictures at an Exhibition*, but by early May he had produced just one movement, the concluding 'Great Gate of Kyev'. 'I started at the end, because it's the least interesting movement to orchestrate,' he wrote to Koussevitsky. 'But you wouldn't believe how much work an easy job can create! The rest will go much faster.'²⁸ The spring, however, had been swallowed up by concerts, the London trip and some Conservatoire examining; only in Lyons-la-Forêt was Ravel at last able to complete the project.

As light relief, Ravel also made a happy contribution to another *Revue musicale* tribute, this time in honour of Gabriel Fauré. As with *Menuet sur le nom d'Haydn* of 1909, contributors had been invited to respond to a melodic motif derived from the letters of the honorand's name. Ravel's contribution was the tender *Berceuse sur le nom de Fauré* for violin and piano, dedicated not to his teacher but to the newborn son of Roland-Manuel and his wife, Suzanne, who were also in residence at Lyons-la-Forêt. The couple had lost a baby two years earlier, so little Claude was welcomed with special joy and the dedication gratefully received. Fauré too was eloquent in his thanks, writing on 15 October, 'I am happier than you can imagine in the place you have attained, so brilliantly and so rapidly. It brings your old professor much joy and pride.'²⁹

Pictures at an Exhibition completed, Ravel embarked on another round of touring, to Holland and Italy. 'For five months I've done nothing but travel and I've not been home more than a week at a time,' he wrote to Alfred Françaix in January 1923, and, exhaustedly to Georgette Marnold a few weeks later, 'These comings and goings are starting to do me in.'³⁰ It was not the best moment for the

At work orchestrating Modest Musorgsky's *Pictures at an Exhibition* at Villa Le Frêne (home of Mme Fernand Dreyfus, mother of Roland-Manuel) in Lyons-la-Forêt, August–September 1922.

pianist E. Robert Schmitz, writing on behalf of his Franco-American Music Society (later Pro Musica), to propose an American tour. Ravel took two months to respond, delayed by another trip to Italy and Britain. 'Excuse me for hesitating,' he eventually replied on 14 March. 'I've not yet given up hope of being able to get back to work, and although success would be very flattering, it doesn't seem to me to be worth the loss of 3 or 4 months.'[31] Negotiations would bounce back and forth for several years, until in 1927 Ravel finally committed himself to a tour.

By this time, Ravel could not hope to attend all the concerts to which he was invited or accept all the engagements he was offered. Increasingly, he participated only in all- (or mostly) Ravel affairs, for which his own contributions typically entailed a handful of his easier piano pieces and the accompaniment of his songs. Never inclined to exert himself with excessive practice, as Ravel aged his playing became stiffer and more faulty. 'I don't think my performance of the *Sonatine* would enhance the programme, since I play it very badly,' he wrote to the organizers of a 'Ravel Festival' in Lausanne in 1926.[32] Several collaborators and auditors recalled his tendency to skate over trickier passages, occasional handfuls of wrong notes and a 'fidgety' approach to the instrument. (Others, though, drew attention to his rhythmic vigour and musically authoritative execution.) In the later 1920s some of his more error-strewn performances – notably of his Violin Sonata, on the American tour – suggest the creeping shadow of ataxia, coupled with exhaustion. Harry Adaskin, who turned pages for Ravel at a concert with Joseph Szigeti in New York in January 1928, recalled that the composer, perhaps overcome by nerves, began the Sonata's *Moto perpetuo* finale so fast that Szigeti's bow became entangled in his strings. 'He never did this at rehearsal!', the horrified violinist panted to Adaskin as they left the stage.[33]

On foreign tours Ravel was frequently invited to conduct his orchestral works, a role that came less naturally still. After a concert in London's Queen's Hall in April 1923, he wrote to Jourdan-Morhange, 'according to the papers I am, if not a *great*, at least a *good* conductor. It's more than I expected!'[34] And indeed he took seven curtain calls – although Sir Henry Wood recalled that he also spent an agonizing twenty minutes of the limited rehearsal time determining how many string desks he would need for *Ma mère l'Oye*. Roger Nichols notes that it was something of a running joke among his close friends as to whether Ravel was a worse pianist or conductor.[35] He was certainly neither fluid nor particularly expressive on the podium, businesslike if occasionally haphazard in his baton technique. On one occasion in the late 1920s he decided to conduct a Viennese performance of *Chansons madécasses*, but created such chaos that the performers decided quietly to ignore him altogether.[36]

The singer Madeleine Grey remembered Ravel as a 'delightful' travelling companion, playful and courteous. But he was demanding and chaotic, too. More than once he was on the point of departure when he realized that his passport had expired; more than once there was a mad dash for a station or concert hall after crucial items of clothing were discovered to have been left in hotel rooms. His spectacles had to be sent back to Montfort from London after one trip; on another he missed a concert when, after a series of sleepless nights, he took a sleeping tablet and did not wake in time. Grey also left a vivid description of the insomniac composer talking incessantly through a night journey in Spain, as she tried desperately to rest.[37]

Tours additionally entailed rounds of press interviews, in which Ravel's opinions were sought on modern music and anything else that crossed his interlocutor's mind, from the League of Nations to local cuisine. He would regularly name Schoenberg as the most important living non-French composer, but consistently highlighted the importance of Stravinsky and Satie for their influence on the younger French generation: Schoenberg, for all his revolutionary significance, had 'too little affinity with the French mind'.[38] For himself, Ravel – still carefully distancing himself from Debussy – offered Mozart and Chabrier as his idols, a pairing of Classical restraint and earthy, jocund audacity well suited to the *esprit du temps*. He also regularly cited Edgar Allan Poe as a key influence, claiming him (in a Madrid interview in 1924) as his 'teacher in

Ravel as conductor, Queen's Hall, London, 14 April 1923.

composition [. . .] Poe taught me that true art is a perfect balance between pure intellect and emotion.'[39] As a literary rather than musical predecessor, Poe too offered a legacy without threat or shadow.

In an article published in *The Star* during a trip to London in October 1923, Ravel appears as

> A little man with a keen, intellectual face, and hair, just going grey, brushed back, wearing a blue shirt with a big soft blue collar, a light brown Norfolk jacket, and purple slippers, and talking French with great volubility [. . .] 'I haven't composed a note for two years [. . .] people don't leave me alone in Paris. Authors, composers, conductors all seem to be pursuing me, so I hide in the forest to escape them.'[40]

It was not quite true that Ravel had written nothing for two years. The Sonata for Violin and Cello had been completed some eighteen months previously, the *Berceuse* was barely a year old, *Pictures at an Exhibition* had been no small undertaking, and in December 1922 he had found time to orchestrate Debussy's 'Sarabande' (from *Pour le piano*) and 'Danse' (*Tarantelle styrienne*) on a commission from the publisher Jobert. But the first half of 1923 had indisputably been a compositional blank. The first hints of a new project emerged only that July, in an interview with *Nouvelles littéraires* that floated a prospective Sonata for Violin and Piano and a piano concerto. (The latter was to be a fantasy on Alain-Fournier's *Le Grand Meaulnes*, which Ravel had been contemplating since reading the novel in hospital in 1916.) But just as he was preparing to begin work on the Sonata, Ravel badly injured two fingers by jamming them in a folding chair. It was months before he could use his hand freely again, a serious impediment for a composer who preferred to work at the piano. 'Should I renounce my virtuoso career?', he wrote ironically to Ida Godebska. 'In any case I'm taking precautions: the piano part of the Sonata for Piano and Violin, which I set to work on yesterday, will be easy.'[41] Unsurprisingly, the Sonata – whose piano part is *not* easy – soon found itself *en panne* (broken down).

In September 1923 Ravel managed to churn out a few pages of piano music for a portmanteau ballet planned by Sonia Pavlov of the Opéra-Comique. *Le Portrait de l'Infante* was to comprise his various 'Spanish' pieces – *Rapsodie espagnole*, *Pavane*, *Alborada*

– with some linking material, but there is no sign that he got as far as orchestrating his 'joins', and the ballet appears never to have been performed.[42] Instead, the autumn vanished in more touring, and when he was finally able to sequester himself in Le Belvédère for the winter, exhaustion and his usual end-of-year depression overtook him. To Manuel de Falla he wrote on 11 January 1924, 'I'd thought to finish my Sonata for Violin and Piano in the first few days of February but I've given up on that [. . .] the blues have returned marvellously.'[43]

Somewhat to his own surprise, if Ravel hadn't made progress on the Sonata, he had managed to complete a Pierre de Ronsard setting for another *Revue musicale* special issue, marking the 400th anniversary of the poet's birth. 'Prunières will be delighted [. . .] I'd told him there was only a slight chance that I'd be able to contribute,' he confided to Falla, admitting that his chosen poem 'corresponds with my state of mind'. *Ronsard à son âme*, however, is a little jewel among Ravel's songs, elegiac and deceptively simple. The composer later joked that he liked it because, with the piano part mostly confined to bare, modal fifths, he could keep one hand free for his cigarette.[44]

By mid-February 1924 Ravel's depression had eased a little, but the Sonata was still stuck and another piece was urgently needed to make up a programme to be given with d'Arányi in London in April. 'What trouble your damned Sonata has given me!' he complained to Jourdan-Morhange on 27 March. 'So I've left it – just for now, of course. And, because it wouldn't be kind to put Arányi to all this inconvenience just for the *Berceuse*, I've decided to write her a *Tzigane*.'[45] With the memory of d'Arányi's extempore virtuosity in his ears and a score of Liszt's *Hungarian Rhapsodies* to hand, he was soon hard at work. Jourdan-Morhange was summoned post-haste to Montfort 'with my violin and the Paganini *Caprices*', and Ravel assured d'Arányi that 'Certain passages will have a really brilliant effect, so long as it's possible to actually play them, something of which I'm not yet quite certain.'[46]

Ravel was still copying and correcting when he reached London in late April, a few days before the first performance of *Tzigane* was given on the 26th. D'Arányi was heroically unfazed: when she came to Paris for the orchestral premiere six months later she even introduced some flourishes of her own, including what she termed 'a glissando with trills'. Ravel was uncharacteristically accommodating, admitting to a friend, 'I don't know what she's doing, but I like it.'[47] His amused permission reflects the nature of *Tzigane*, which is located firmly in nineteenth-century traditions of virtuoso performance. For once, the composer was happy to accede to the 'game' of making a work of vertiginous difficulty more diabolical still.

After yet more touring (to Spain and Belgium), by 5 June Ravel was back in Montfort and contemplating with no little anxiety the tasks that lay before him. 'Please excuse me, both of you: an opera and a sonata to get done by the end of the year: I'm not shifting any more,' he wrote to the singer Marcelle Gerar.[48] After years of prevarication, he had at last turned his attention to Colette's 'fairy-ballet' – soon to be rechristened *L'Enfant et les sortilèges*.

The collaboration between Ravel and Colette was one of the decade's more unexpected meetings of artistic minds. Reviewing the eventual premiere of their opera, the critic Raymond Balliman would write, 'The union of poetry and music is such that it is impossible to separate the collaborators'; of the Opéra production in 1939, the critic Carol-Bérard reflected, 'Was not Ravel the musician whose heart could best understand Colette's heart? Was it not he who could follow her most gracefully into the kingdom of dreams?'[49] And yet, while in 1926 Roland-Manuel memorably evoked 'this enchantress collaborating with this illusionist', he would later write, 'One would look in vain for two more original spirits. One would be hard put to find two more incompatible.'[50]

The best-known account of the genesis of *L'Enfant* was set down by Colette herself. In the lyrical 1939 essay 'Un salon en 1900' she depicts a distant, mysterious composer who took her libretto and vanished, emerging 'five years later' with a completed score:

> Ravel did not treat me with any privilege, explaining nothing nor granting me an early hearing. He seemed to concern himself

only with the duo of the two Cats, asking gravely if I minded if he replaced 'mouâu' with 'mouain', or perhaps it was the other way around.[51]

In truth, however, there was considerably more interaction than this gracefully elided portrait allowed. When Ravel wrote to Colette about her *Divertissement pour ma fille* in 1919, he headed his letter 'Chère Madame', but by 1924 his salutation had become 'Chère amie'.[52]

Despite their vastly different public personas, in some respects this flamboyant writer and the deeply private composer were oddly akin. Both were storytellers and keen observers of the natural world, which they regarded with amusement, wonder and affection. Like Ravel, Colette prized tautness and grace, tenderness and sparkling wit. Her prose evinces a composer's sense of metre and cadence: 'Musical contours and the [written] phrase are born of the same elusive and immortal pair – sound and rhythm,' she wrote in 1936.[53] Jourdan-Morhange, a close mutual friend, observed that Ravel and Colette shared an 'artisan's care for perfecting their work'.[54] 'One gives birth away from the flame, and with calculation,' wrote Colette, echoing Ravel's assertion that he composed with the intellectual detachment that Poe expounded in 'The Philosophy of Composition' (like Ravel, Colette reportedly 'read and re-read Edgar Allan Poe in Baudelaire's translation').[55] And, crucially, both artists were profoundly influenced by unusually close relationships with their mothers, and were mourning their loss; for both, *L'Enfant et les sortilèges* would represent a loving and poignant *tombeau*.

Colette had drafted her libretto in 1916, on the commission of Jacques Rouché (by now director of the Opéra de Paris), who had offered it first to Paul Dukas and Stravinsky before approaching Ravel. Having accepted the libretto in 1917, in February 1919 Ravel had reported to Colette from Megève that he was

> thinking of some modifications . . . Don't be afraid, they're not cuts – on the contrary. For example, couldn't the squirrel's tale

be developed? Imagine all that a squirrel could say of the forest, and how that could be expressed in music! Another thing: what would you think of the cup and the teapot, in old Wedgwood – black – singing a ragtime? I confess I'm delighted by the prospect of having a ragtime sung by two Negroes at the Académie nationale de musique [the Opéra].[56]

Colette responded quickly, in a letter of striking warmth and ease:

But certainly, a ragtime! But of course, Negroes in Wedgwood! May a terrific gust from the music hall blow off the dust of the Opéra! Go for it! I'm happy to hear that you are still thinking about *Divertissement pour ma fille*, I despaired of you, and I'd heard that you were ill [. . .] And the squirrel will say all that you wish. Does the 'cat' duo, exclusively miaowed, please you? We'll get acrobats. Isn't the Arithmetic business a polka? I wish you good health and shake your hand impatiently.[57]

In the summer of 1920 Ravel was still thinking about the opera. 'Some inside information', he wrote to Roland-Manuel: 'I can assure you that this work, in two parts, will be notable for its mixture of styles, which will be severely criticized; this leaves Colette indifferent and me not giving a d[amn].'[58]

Only in the late spring of 1924, however, did Ravel set to work in earnest, spurred on by the prospect of a premiere early in 1925 – not in Paris, but at Raoul Gunsbourg's Opéra de Monte-Carlo, with Diaghilev's Ballets Russes. 'It's going better. I'd really believed that the magneto was buggered,' he reported on 26 August. 'It's not yet the Blue Train, nor the Stockholm express, nor even the new 6-horsepower Delage [car], but it's moving.'[59] Although the autumn was spent in frantic activity, by Christmas Ravel was getting desperate. 'I still have a little hope, but so little!', he lamented to Lucien Garban on 17 December, and three days after Christmas he wrote to Roland-Manuel excusing himself from the end-of-year festivities: '[I beg you] to forget neither Gunsbourg nor myself in your prayers.' Even his correspondence then ceased, until on

18 January 1925 he surfaced with a brief, relieved note to his editor: 'the composition is finished, the transcription almost complete: I'm copying.'[60]

Few theatrical works better capture the zeitgeist of the 1920s than *L'Enfant et les sortilèges*, in its blending of song and dance, popular music and pastiche, and its richly varied but pared-down orchestral textures (more than one critic was to invoke the *style dépouillé*). Its dialogues of destruction and reparation, determined modernism and painful nostalgia also speak powerfully to the preoccupations of the post-war years. These sweeping themes are focused through the small central figure of the Child, who is found, as the curtain rises, stuck at his desk and fed up with his lessons. His mother enters and reproaches him for his laziness; his only response is to stick out his tongue, and he is condemned to his room until dinnertime. After Maman leaves, the furious Child rushes around his room destroying everything he can get his hands on, accompanied by bitonal flurries in the winds. But as he sinks, 'satiated with devastation', into an armchair, 'O surprise!' The chair, 'hobbling like an enormous toad', gets up and walks away. One by one all the injured objects come to life, reproaching the Child for his destructive acts.

'There's a bit of everything in [*L'Enfant*],' Ravel said. 'You'll see ... there's Massenet, Puccini [. . .] American [jazz and operetta] and Monteverdi!'[61] The lumbering armchairs dance a minuet in the style of Louis xv; the Clock's mechanism runs down like Offenbach's doll; and the swaggering foxtrot of the Wedgwood Teapot – in the 'black' key of G-flat major – merges with the F-major *chinoiseries* of the Teacup. The Fire emerges in swirling Donizettian coloratura, and the Shepherds and Shepherdesses of the mutilated wallpaper dance a pastorale to the tambour and drone bass. With the 'adorable fairytale Princess' of his torn storybook the Child sings an impassioned duet (here are the Puccinian echoes), before lamenting her disappearance in a brief and poignant little aria that takes a lead from Massenet's 'Adieu, notre petite table' (*Manon*). 'A little old man' (Arithmetic personified) and his chorus of Numbers then appear, beating out a chant of impossible sums in manic parody of the catalogue aria.

The raunchy meowed duet of the two Cats leads the Child into the starlit Garden, where, in a ravishing chain of waltzes, the Dragonfly, Bat, Frogs and Squirrel confront him with more reminders of the havoc he has wrought. Lonely and afraid, the Child calls for his mother, rousing the fury of the animals. In their frenzy a little squirrel is injured, and the Child binds up the wounded paw before falling back weakly. Suddenly, there is a 'profound silence, stupor' among the creatures, and as a hesitant, tripping bassline moves up through the orchestra, they try to repeat the word the Child has sobbed: 'Maman!' A light appears in the window and Maman's first entry is recalled by the full orchestra as they bear the Child towards the house, singing a gentle fugal chorus in his praise. The wandering oboe melody of the opera's opening returns, now doubled by two violins and anchored firmly in the major mode. As the Child stretches his arms towards his mother in loving relief, the audience too can exhale at last.

The premiere of *L'Enfant et les sortilèges*, which took place on 21 March 1925, was not without incident. A few days beforehand Ravel precipitated a crisis when, encountering Diaghilev in the foyer of his hotel, he refused to shake his hand: the rejection of *La Valse*, it appeared, was still raw. Diaghilev, whose company had been seasonally resident in Monte Carlo since 1922, was then embroiled in a long-standing campaign to undermine Gunsbourg and install himself as the theatre's director. Seizing on Ravel's snub, he immediately withdrew his dancers from rehearsal on the grounds that the score of *L'Enfant* was 'too difficult'. René Léon, who oversaw the governing body of the Opéra de Monte-Carlo, called his bluff. 'It is exceedingly strange that these difficulties should have arisen just a few hours after an incident that apparently took place with M. Ravel in the lobby of the Hôtel de Paris,' he wrote tartly, 'after which you appear to have declared, in the presence of several witnesses, "I will not be forced to dance in his opera".'[62] Only after a tense exchange of correspondence was Diaghilev compelled to set his dancers to work again, on pain of losing his contract.

Despite these machinations, *L'Enfant* was a triumph. André Corneau, in a rapturous review in the *Journal de Monaco*, wrote that

'M. Ravel was the object of prolonged ovations, when, from the heights of the royal box, he appeared three times [. . .] to bow to the audience.'[63] When the opera opened in Paris the following February – not at Rouché's Opéra, for reasons that remain obscure, but at the Opéra-Comique – it met with a more tumultuous reception. Ravel, who had embarked on an extended tour to Scandinavia, Britain and Belgium, had to rely on his friends for an account of the premiere, which Roland-Manuel dutifully provided. Although 'the family circle naturally applauds', he wrote,

> The Institut has damned you to the seventh generation [. . .] You're played every evening amid the heady atmosphere of a scandal. As this never goes as far as preventing the music from being heard, everyone is congratulating one another, especially the performers. 'We're having fun,' Roger Bourdin [who played the Clock and the Cat] confided to me, 'we're living through historic moments.'[64]

'The modernists applaud and boo the others,' wrote Colette to her daughter, 'and during the "miaowed" duet the racket is dreadful.'[65] But if Parisian audiences were eager participants in the traditional sport of livening up theatrical proceedings, the balance of critical opinion had now tilted firmly in Ravel's favour. Although one review stated blandly that 'It is difficult for us to feel any interest in a drama where the protagonists start off as different bits of the furniture,' and the elderly André Messager repeated the old trope of the *pince-sans-rire* ('don't demand any emotion of him, still less any tenderness'), Maurice Le Boucher spoke for many when he concluded that the opera's ending, despite its 'spareness of means', was so beautiful that it made one weep.[66]

'I feel I've aged 10 years,' Ravel wrote exhaustedly to Jacques Durand from Montfort after the Monte Carlo premiere. 'It's always like that after every job. Lucky for me I've produced so little!' But he had little opportunity to reflect on either his opera or his fiftieth birthday, which he had marked on 7 March 1925. 'The American commission,' he promised. 'I'm counting on getting to it tomorrow.'[67]

The 'American commission', from the philanthropist Elizabeth Sprague Coolidge, was for a cycle of songs on texts of the composer's choice, accompanied, if possible, by flute, cello and piano. Browsing the booksellers' stalls along the Seine, Ravel had discovered Évariste Parny's collection *Chansons madécasses* (1787), and was instantly hooked by its heady blend of eroticism and radical Enlightenment politics.[68] In his prefatory 'Avertissement' Parny had written of the warring Malagasy peoples, their conflicts driven by the demands of European slave-traders: 'without us,' he observed, 'these people would be calm and content.' Those words were still resonating in May 1925 when Ravel's 'Aoua!' (the only song then completed) was given a first private performance. France was then at the height of a conflict with another of its African colonial possessions, Morocco, and the emphatic line 'Méfiez-vous des blancs!' ('Beware of the white men!') prompted the composer Léon Moreau to heckle loudly and storm out.[69] The song's titular cry, 'Aoua!', does not appear in Parny's poetry: Ravel, always fascinated by language-as-sound, added it himself, a dramatic vocal colour that sits compellingly alongside the cello glissandi and the flute's startling *quasi tromba* (like a trumpet). Compositionally, the bitonal opposition of 'black notes', in the effective D-sharp minor of the voice and piano right hand, against the 'white notes' of the cello's open strings and piano left hand, is a potent visual, as well as aural, effect.

In the spring of 1926 Ravel managed to complete the outer two songs, 'Nahandove' and 'Il est doux', working as usual up to the frantic last minute before the premiere on 8 May in Rome. Both songs are crafted with a linearity and *dépouillé* restraint that stand in deliberate, provocative contrast with the luscious eroticism of their texts. In 'Nahandove' it is the gradual accumulation of sound that propels the music towards what is in every sense a climax; in the opening bars of 'Il est doux', Ravel's reluctance to employ the harmonic heft of the piano brings a coolness and distance in which the sensual and dramatic fervour of the first two songs can dissipate. The final bars, as Nichols notes, recall the conclusion of 'Le Grillon' (*Histoires naturelles*), two D-flat major endings with a sudden, almost cinematic 'pull-back' to a nocturnal landscape; the vocal lines in both songs also curve upwards from the tonic via a Lydian G♮.⁷⁰ But where the last bars of 'Le Grillon' move through a fully articulated harmonic progression, 'Il est doux' offers just a bare fifth in the piano, and even this dissolves in the final three bars, whisking the tonal rug out from beneath the final, offhand command ('Allez, et préparez le repas' – 'Go and prepare the meal').

Chansons madécasses complete, Ravel returned once more to his Violin Sonata. Inevitably, it was a new fixed date for a premiere, at the end of May 1927, that finally jolted him into action: 'this time, I'm committed!' he wrote firmly.⁷¹ Equally inevitably, he ran down the clock, writing to Gerar on 21 April, 'May it please our good Euterpe that our Sonata will be almost complete [by 23 May], and that Enescu won't be sightreading it a week later.' Five days later he complained that her petitions must have been half-hearted – 'Let's proceed to human sacrifices' – but he managed to finish the Sonata just in time.⁷²

As so often, Ravel was fortunate in his interpreter. According to the recollection of a young Yehudi Menuhin, George Enescu read the sonata for the first time on the day of the concert, when he and Ravel played it to Durand; he then immediately played it over

With friends and collaborators Luc-Albert Moreau, Hélène Jourdan-Morhange, Madeleine Grey, Germaine Malançon and Jacques de Zogheb, 1925.

again – from memory.[73] But the eleven-year-old Menuhin may not have been aware of other rehearsals. Manuel Rosenthal, who had then been studying with Ravel for about a year, talked of 'difficult rehearsals' and indeed asserted that Ravel had completed an entirely different third movement, which Enescu had played through, but which the composer had then destroyed. 'Is the new finale as good?' Rosenthal had asked, contemplating the pile of ashes in the fireplace. 'Oh no, I like it much less. But its form is much better suited to the Sonata as a whole.'[74]

In his 'Autobiographical Sketch' Ravel would draw attention to the 'two essentially incompatible instruments' of the Sonata for Violin and Piano: 'far from balancing their contrasts, I draw attention to their incompatibility.' The first movement lies close to the Sonata for Violin and Cello in its intensely conversational – sometimes even combative – play of timbres. It is followed by the remarkable 'Blues', a movement so intertwined with the spirit of the age that, as Deborah Mawer observes, it seems to prefigure Billy Mayerl's popular *Marigold* (1927) and even Gershwin's 'Summertime' (1935).[75] Ravel was vocal in his appreciation of jazz and blues, both as an expression of a uniquely American culture ('take jazz seriously!', he declared in several interviews), and as a richly mutable source of inspiration for contemporary art music more generally. 'While I adopted this popular form of your music,' he would say to his American audience in his 1928 lecture on 'Contemporary Music', 'I venture to say that nevertheless it is French music, Ravel's music, that I have written.'[76]

Ravel's compositional accounting of his Violin Sonata is remarkably consistent across his public and private writing, and throughout the work's long gestation. In November 1923 he told the composer Jean Huré, 'the form, character and style have all been fixed for a month, but I don't have the themes. I hope that this lacuna will soon be filled. Then I'll have nothing more to do than to write this *Sonata*: that won't take long.'[77] In a Danish interview published a few months later, he similarly explained, 'I have not yet written a single note of my new sonata, and only a few days ago I found the theme of the first movement. But the sonata is composed, nevertheless.'[78] In 1928 he would declare to *The Chesterian*, 'I had already determined [the Sonata's] rather unusual form, the manner of writing for the instruments, and even the character of the themes for each of the three movements, before "inspiration" had begun to prompt any of those themes.'[79] (Of *Tzigane* he wrote similarly to Robert Casadesus in April 1924, 'apart from a few bars, it's completely done – the form isn't complicated anyway – but almost nothing is written.'[80])

Elsewhere Ravel drew a hopeful parallel between his practice and Mozart's, pointing out that for Mozart, too, the compositional act could be essentially cerebral, the committing of a score to paper sometimes no more than the almost mechanical realization of a drawn-out internal process.[81] While he had perhaps been compelled to accept 'not writing notes' as a necessary (if frustrating) stage of the compositional process, his articulation of his methods in the 1920s also drew consciously closer to the rationale Poe offered in 'The Philosophy of Composition'. Poe suggested there that the famous refrain of 'The Raven' ('Nevermore!') had been determined by reducing the possible options to a single, inevitable choice, the one word that, by its sonorous qualities and shades of meaning, could possibly fit the complex poetic matrix. In these grinding post-war years Ravel was able to get the compositional machine turning again through a conscious philosophy of masterly, relentless *choosing*. 'Inspiration – I don't know what you mean by that,' he once told the violinist André Asselin as they were rehearsing the Violin Sonata. 'What is most difficult for a composer is choice, yes, choice.'[82]

6
Dissolving

'My little Édouard,' wrote the elder Ravel brother on 13 January 1928, 'If I return to Europe alive, it will prove that I am hard to kill!' Nine days earlier Maurice had arrived in New York on the ss *France* to begin a long-awaited American tour. A decade of post-war European renown had in no way prepared him for the reception he encountered:

> As soon as we arrived in the harbour, a cloud of journalists invaded the boat, with cameras, movie cameras, sketch artists. I had to escape them for a minute so I could see the entry into harbour – even then it was a bit late, but splendid in any case. My stay in New York (4 days that have seemed to last 4 months) hasn't even allowed me time to work at the piano a little: ever since I was installed at the Hotel Langdon – a small hotel, comprising only 12 storeys (I'm on the 8th) – and delightfully comfortable (a whole apartment), the telephone hasn't stopped. Every instant someone brings me baskets of flowers, or the most delicious fruit in the world. Rehearsals, teams of journalists [. . .] relieving each other every hour, letters, invitations to which my manager responds for me, receptions. Evening, rest: dancing, Black theatres, giant cinemas, etc. [. . .] I even made a film, with make-up 2 cm thick. I forgot the concert that the Boston Symphony gave in New York devoted to my music. They made me appear on stage: an audience of 3,500 on their feet. Extraordinary ovation.[1]

Alexandre Tansman, who shared the composer's box at that Boston Symphony concert, recalled that the audience's response had moved Ravel to tears: 'This would never happen to me in Europe,' he said.[2]

Robert Schmitz had originally proposed that the centrepiece of the tour should be Ravel himself appearing as soloist in a newly composed piano concerto. This plan had swiftly been abandoned, the concerto proving intractable; instead, Ravel committed only to conducting, and to performing his limited repertoire of piano and chamber works. In the course of his four-month tour he would appear in about thirty concerts; conduct the Boston, Chicago, Cleveland and San Francisco Symphony Orchestras; hear George Gershwin play and sit in on a recording session with the 'king of jazz' Paul Whiteman and his orchestra; meet Fritz Kreisler, Mary Pickford and Douglas Fairbanks; visit Niagara Falls, the Grand Canyon and Edgar Allan Poe's house; and rattle across more than 29,000 kilometres (18,000 mi.) of railway. 'Oh yes, oh yes, I'm a great success, but dear God it's exhausting!' he wrote to Ida Godebska en route from Portland to Denver.[3]

Ravel was entranced by the Californian scenery, which he described at length in several letters. The Grand Canyon, however, left him lost for words: 'you'll just have to go,' he told Cipa. A seven-hour stopover in Omaha was spent visiting a jazz club; in Detroit he toured the Ford factory, sending a dutiful account home to Édouard. Some elder-brotherly admonitions also sailed back across the Atlantic: 'I've heard from everyone except you,' he complained from Los Angeles, and to Hélène Jourdan-Morhange a few days later, 'I hope my brother is still alive.' Apart from anything else, he needed Édouard to sort out a new vacuum cleaner for Le Belvédère, having been particularly taken with one he'd seen in the Parisian hotel he usually patronized. 'Have you done anything about the vacuum cleaner yet?', he asked on 13 March, from somewhere along the Mississippi.[4]

Despite the bewildering inefficiencies of his route – he made four separate trips to Canada, travelled from San Francisco to Seattle via Los Angeles, and reached Buffalo, NY, via a monumental loop through New Orleans, Houston and Phoenix – by early April Ravel

On board the ss *France*, with the Ukrainian-American lyric soprano Nina Koshetz, January 1928.

was writing to Mme Dreyfus, 'I've never been better than during this crazy tour. I've finally worked out the reason: I've never lived such a rational existence.' After years of insomnia, he had discovered that on American trains he was able to sleep, a newfound capacity that he would document with delighted astonishment in many letters ('slept last night and today, before and after lunch'; 'slept 9 hours'; 'slept almost without interruption for 2 days and 2 nights').[5]

Although not even Ravel's celebrity could mask his increasingly haphazard pianism, his concerts were overwhelmingly successful. Above all, the American reporters and public were charmed by the man himself, small, startlingly stylish, buzzing with energy and uncompromisingly French. The *Buffalo Evening News* (17 April) introduced him as a 'dynamic little man' who claimed to walk 10 kilometres (6 mi.) daily and paced the room for the duration of the interview. The *Musical Courier* (26 January) wrote of his 'definite, incisive way of expressing himself', noting that 'he appears to be inclined to take things from their humorous side.' The *Houston Post-Dispatch*, meanwhile, ran with the memorable headline 'Reporters Mourn Lack of French as Maurice Ravel Talks about Jazz and U.S. in Native Tongue' (8 April).

When Ravel returned home at the end of April, the demands of his *boulot* made themselves quickly and insistently felt. Among the letters that had piled up in Montfort was a note from the dancer and impresario Ida Rubinstein: 'I'm impatiently awaiting your return so we can speak again about this fine project, which you've promised to complete for me by the autumn.'[6] Rubinstein's commission was for a Spanish ballet, its score to be compiled and orchestrated from Isaac Albéniz's great piano cycle *Iberia*. In the early summer Ravel, in Saint-Jean-de-Luz, was just getting underway when a chance encounter with the Cuban-Spanish composer Joaquín Nin upended his plans. Portions of *Iberia*, Nin pointed out, had already been orchestrated by Enrique Fernández Arbós, to whom Albéniz's heirs had reserved exclusive rights. 'Who is this Arbós?!', Nin recalled Ravel expostulating furiously. 'And what am I going to tell Ida?'[7] A frantic exchange of correspondence quickly confirmed Nin's information, and Ravel hastened back to Paris to

'L'Impromptu du Belvédère', 10 June 1928. Ravel (gesticulating) sits at right, with Joaquín Nin on his right and Jane Bathori on his left. The party was organized by Marcelle Gerar to celebrate the success of the American tour and unveil Léon Leyritz's bust of Ravel. The festivities continued into the small hours, ending at a jazz club in Versailles.

devise an alternative plan with Rubinstein. He returned to Saint-Jean-de-Luz newly committed, as he wrote to Georgette Marnold, to 'a machine' that he'd been contemplating for three years but had 'never executed, afraid of botching it [. . .] It will be: no music, no composition: only orchestral effect.'[8] By 27 August the title of the new ballet was confirmed: having tried and rejected *Fandango*, Ravel had settled on *Boléro*.

Jacques Durand was delighted with the change of plan. It was much more fitting, he felt, that a composer of Ravel's stature should write a new ballet than arrange someone else's work. In a letter of 13 August Durand pushed hard to negotiate favourable terms, mindful of Rubinstein's stipulation of a one-year embargo on concert performances and a three-year block on any other staged production. Nine days later he suffered a stroke and died, aged 63. Durand's steadfast support, probity and professionalism had sustained Ravel's career for almost 25 years. In his last days he had helped to secure both Ravel's fortune and his firm's financial standing. *Boléro* was to become the century's most unexpected musical hit. Within months of the first concert performances, it was being described in reviews as 'the famous *Boléro*', the hall so packed that the critics could barely squeeze in.[9] By 1937, to Ravel's utter astonishment, some 50,000 copies of the piano transcription had flown out of Durand's warehouse.[10]

There is, as Ravel happily admitted, nothing really 'Spanish' about *Boléro*: its remorseless rhythms perhaps owe more to the rat-ta-ta-tat of the American trains that had for months been drumming in his ears. Rather, it is a study in insistence, and a practical treatise in orchestration. Unexpected instrumental timbres abound, from the oboe d'amore to the piccolo clarinet, the saxophones in the second rotation of the second, more chromatic, melodic strand, and the stratospheric trombone solo in the third. More remarkable still is the third rotation of the first (diatonic) half of the theme, in which the piccolos shrilly double the melody in G and E major, above the solo horn and celesta in C: the effect is less of polytonality than a slightly out-of-tune fairground organ.

The ballet premiere of *Boléro*, which took place on 22 November 1928, was 'very successful', Ravel wrote – 'though picturesque, which it shouldn't have been'.[11] There was, he felt, too much Spain and not enough 'machine'. In a 1932 interview he would declare, 'It was a factory which inspired my *Boléro*. I would like it always to be played with a vast factory in the background.'[12] Édouard Ravel asserted that his brother even had a particular building in mind, and that when travelling through the western outskirts of Paris he would always point out 'the *Boléro* factory'.[13] But for all his delight in the machines themselves, Édouard stressed that Ravel 'would always come out marvelling and obsessed by the automated movements of all the workers'. His fascination was not just that of the engineer but of the artist, his inspiration drawn to the spaces between cool automation and warm humanity. The great, slow crescendo of *Boléro* is an accumulation not just of volume and sonority but of dissonance, structural tension and visceral emotion. As in *La Valse*, the final release – the plummet from an unsustainable E major back into the tonic C, the disintegration of the melody beneath the triumphant ostinato – represents both the breakdown of the machine and a very human capitulation.

Ravel responded to the wild popularity of *Boléro* with ironic bemusement. When the conductor Ernest Ansermet claimed to find the work very good, he responded, 'I can't think why'; elsewhere, he famously described it as 'a piece for orchestra without music'.[14] He was reportedly charmed by a Montfort acquaintance who had Ravel's own recording (made with the Orchestre Lamoureux in January 1930) on a pair of 78s and often listened to the first disc but never the second, explaining, 'it's not worth listening to the other one, it's the same thing!'[15] Nevertheless, in a 1931 interview Ravel would describe *Boléro* as 'the work in which he had most completely attained his specified purpose'.[16] And for all his self-deprecation, he was unashamedly delighted when, passing a building site the day after a radio broadcast of *Boléro*, he heard three construction workers whistling his tune.[17]

The six months that followed the completion of *Boléro* were almost as relentless as the American tour. A few days before

Ravel with Ida Rubinstein and the cast of *Boléro*, Vienna, 1929.

dispatching the finished score, Ravel sat down with Roland-Manuel to dictate the text known as his 'Esquisse autobiographique' (Autobiographical Sketch) for the Aeolian Company. His punishing schedule offered a ready excuse for his failure ever to review and revise Roland-Manuel's notes, and the 'Sketch' went unpublished until the 'Hommage à Ravel' issue of *La Revue musicale* in 1938 (Roland-Manuel's introduction to the text there begins by stressing that 'Ravel hated speaking about himself'). On 16 October Ravel signed a contract for *Boléro* then departed for London, where he took part in an all-Ravel programme at the Aeolian Hall three days later. On 23 October he was in Oxford, where he was awarded the degree of doctor *honoris causa*. He was, the pianist Gordon Bryan recalled, 'particularly taken' with the pink and white silk gown, which had to be taken up to fit him; the dons, meanwhile, were politely nonplussed by the resplendent waistcoat he sported beneath it.[18]

A subsequent tour of Spain, with Madeleine Grey and the violinist Claude Lévy, was followed in turn by excursions to Geneva and London (again) and two trips to Vienna, first for Rubinstein's staging of *Boléro* and *La Valse*, then for the Austrian premiere of *L'Enfant et les sortilèges*. Back in Paris for a week in early March 1929, Ravel was at the Opéra for the public premiere of the children's ballet *L'Éventail de Jeanne*, to which he had contributed a witty opening 'Fanfare' (the score, completed for a first, private performance in 1927, comprised numbers by ten composers).[19] He also accepted a nomination to the Conservatoire's governing Conseil supérieur, filling the seat left vacant by the recent death of André Messager. But if Ravel had thus finally marked a formal reconciliation with one of the institutions that had so decisively rejected him a quarter of a century earlier, he would energetically decline to lend countenance to the other. A gossipy little note in *Comœdia* (24 May) quotes him as refusing categorically to stand for Messager's vacant seat in the Institut de France, with the declaration, 'I don't believe the Institut has any useful purpose.' In any case, he added, he could not really imagine himself in the mandatory Napoleonic *bicorne*, with its frill of ostrich feathers.

In DMus robes, Oxford, 23 October 1928.

By mid-April 1929 Ravel was back in Montfort and hard at work. 'I'm gestating a Concerto (I'm at the vomiting stage),' he wrote cheerfully to Marie Gaudin, and by September he was sufficiently confident to enter into negotiations for the new work with Serge Koussevitzky.[20] In December, however, he would unhesitatingly reject the conductor's proffered terms, which included a year's exclusive rights to the new concerto. Not only was he planning to premiere his work himself 'on all five continents', he wrote, it was 'far from being finished'. 'As always, I'm working at several things at once: another Concerto, for the left hand, and even, in the last few days, a symphonic poem. This outsider might pip them at the post.'[21]

The 'outsider', a symphonic 'aeroplane in C' titled *Dédale vi* (or 38, 'or 43, or 17: I'm not sure'[22]), would never leave the ground. Instead, by the spring of 1930 Ravel was concentrating firmly on his 'other Concerto'. This was a commission from the Austrian pianist Paul Wittgenstein, who, having lost his right arm in the First World War, had rebuilt his career on repertoire for the left hand alone, soliciting concertos from composers including Hindemith, Korngold and Richard Strauss. Composer and pianist had met in March 1929 at a dinner given by the French ambassador in Vienna. If Ravel, dilatory as ever, had spent the months following their encounter engrossed in his long-contemplated concerto for *two* hands, the negotiations with Koussevitzky would reciprocally be followed by a headlong plunge into the Concerto for Left Hand.

For most of 1930 Ravel would be lured from Le Belvédère only rarely. He oversaw the decoration, in impeccable Art Deco, of a *pied à terre* in Édouard and the Bonnets' new home and factory premises in Levallois; and he sallied forth from Montfort to give Arturo Toscanini a piece of his mind when, in early May, he conducted *Boléro* at the Opéra 'twice as fast' as Ravel had marked it. 'I knew that Toscanini would take *Boléro* at a ridiculous tempo, and wanted to tell him so,' he explained to Godebska; consternation predictably ensued.[23] Then there was an invitation he could hardly refuse: a festival in his honour at Saint-Jean-de-Luz in August, at which the street of his birth was to be renamed the quai Maurice Ravel. On 30 July he complained to Gaudin,

> I'm working, therefore I'm not sleeping – or hardly – four hours without drugs, five and a half with them. And to think that as soon as this Concerto for Left Hand is finished, I'll have to attack the other one! Damned Cibourians, who are going to make me lose a week![24]

Despite his protestations, the Festival Maurice Ravel was a happy success. Although the composer took himself off for a tactful drink during the unveiling of his own memorial plaque ('Not for *anything in the world* would I be present at the ceremony'), he was delighted to preside over the *pelota* championship that followed.[25] And on his return to Montfort, it was with great pride and childlike astonishment that he would inform Jourdan-Morhange, 'Do you know, I have a *quai*! There is a quai Ravel in Ciboure!'[26]

By late September, Ravel – 'working more and more and sleeping less and less' – was finishing the orchestration of his new concerto, and by mid-November he would write relievedly to Roger-Ducasse, 'The Concerto for left hand is finished and the other should be in January. (My facility is renowned.)' But the year's frantic effort had caught up with him, and he had been plunged into one of his periodic states of nervous exhaustion. Under doctors' orders to rest, he abandoned hope of completing the two-handed concerto for the coming season. The winter passed slowly and quietly. 'You're never seen nowadays,' Roland-Manuel wrote in February 1931, gently reminding the composer of 'those who love you dearly'.[27]

By this time Ravel was taking up the Concerto in G again, but only 'very slowly', he wrote, 'can't push it at all.' With the spring his energy returned, and by the summer he was hard at work once more. Since he was also driving himself through a pianistic boot camp in preparation for his projected world tour, his correspondence again fell by the wayside. A letter to Edwin Evans ends with the admonition, 'Above all, don't let anyone else know that I've replied to *you* – that would cause at least 300 dramas!' By late November he had signed off his second concerto in two years – although, as he admitted to Henri Rabaud (who had succeeded Fauré as director of the Paris Conservatoire), 'I'm not far from being

The forest of Rambouillet was Ravel's 'kingdom', wrote Hélène Jourdan-Morhange; 'He knew its every path and clearing.' With Jourdan-Morhange, 1932.

[finished] myself.' He was writing to withdraw from a competition jury ('I fear I'd be asleep as soon as the first candidate begins') and was once again under doctors' orders to rest.[28] Gone was the plan of parading his concerto around 'all five continents'; instead, Marguerite Long was to give the premiere under the composer's baton, and their tour was to be confined to Europe.

While certain structural elements recur in both of Ravel's concertos, and while both betray the influence of jazz and blues and revel in percussive passagework, their models, forms, orchestral dispositions and aesthetic premises are very different. The Concerto for Left Hand is characterized above all by the physical presence of the soloist. To audiences for whom the First World War was a recent memory, Wittgenstein's empty sleeve would inevitably conjure tropes of suffering, loss and resurgence. Ravel's Concerto weaves those themes into an essentially Romantic narrative that demands a pianism of corresponding nineteenth-century virtuosity. It is the Concerto in G, therefore, that pits the soloist against a lighter, synthetically more 'Classical' orchestra, with reduced strings and single winds and brass. The darker, heavier orchestral timbres and the inexorably mounting introduction of the Concerto for Left Hand, by contrast, herald the arrival of a titanic, Lisztian figure – a 'conquering hero', as Long put it.[29]

In musical terms, the Concerto for Left Hand is defined by the tense interplay and eventual fusion of elements that are initially presented as disjunctive. Rather than allowing his contradictions to dissolve across the artificial divides of movement breaks, Ravel weaves them into a single taut arc, folding together elements of sonata form with those of a multi-movement work. Like *La Valse*, whose D-major tonality it shares, the Concerto shudders into existence from the lowest registers of the orchestra on an extended supertonic (E) pedal, which gives way to the tonic only with the piano's reclamation of the opening thematic material at bar 36. (In *La Valse*, the tonic arrives at an equivalent structural moment, with the emergence of the first clear waltz theme.) This opening passage serves as introduction, *maestoso* first movement and – in the lyrical, meditative second subject – slow movement as well. The longer second half of the concerto (from fig. 14) is at once development and recapitulation, scherzo and finale. A long, mechanistic passage, modulatory and relentless, is surmounted by what Ravel termed 'a sort of obstinate chant', its bluesy flattened third derived directly from the opening material. A reprise of the opening leads to an extended cadenza in which 'the various elements that have emerged over the course of the work compete until they are shattered in the final brutal peroration', and a last, fleeting recall of the 'scherzo' material.[30]

Ravel never openly acknowledged the theatricality of the Concerto for Left Hand, instead framing his compositional challenge simply as 'maintain[ing] interest in an extended work with such limited means'.[31] He was equally prosaic when it came to the Concerto in G. While he asserted in several interviews that the opening melody had come to him on the train from Oxford in 1928, he used that anecdote to draw attention not to picturesque inspiration but to craft. To one journalist he stressed that this 'first idea' was 'nothing', agreeing with his interviewer's suggestion that it was only the start of the 'work of chiselling': 'Exactly, and that's the only work that counts.'[32] Hard at work on the Concerto in 1931, Ravel described it as a 'divertissement', a title he later relinquished with the explanation that it was redundant: *divertissement*, he asserted, was integral to the nature of a concerto, which 'should be light-hearted and brilliant, and not aim at profundity or at dramatic effects'.[33] (The Concerto for Left Hand, he conceded in the same interview, was 'much nearer to [. . .] the more solemn kind of traditional Concerto'.) While he offered no musical models for the Concerto for Left Hand, every discussion of the Concerto in G emphasizes its lineage (which he traced above all from Mozart and Saint-Saëns), its clarity and formal strictness.

Although he willingly adopted the language of Classicism, however, Ravel deftly skirted the charge of *neo*classicism. In a 1932 interview that again circles around questions of influence, tradition and style, he goes to great lengths to stress the work's connections with Bach, Mozart and Mendelssohn, but when presented in response with a frame of neoclassicism, can only concede half-heartedly that 'the principle isn't bad.'[34] Discomfited by the construction of pastiche as avant-garde, Ravel had publicly expressed reservations about Stravinsky's neoclassical works, particularly *Mavra* and the Concerto for Piano and Winds. The Concerto in G – like *Le Tombeau de Couperin* – is perhaps better understood in the context of what Andy Fry neatly describes as a 'more organic' neoclassicism, less self-conscious historicization and more natural progression.[35]

The opening *Allegramente* ('of strictly classical design'[36]) traces a similar initial template to that of Mozart's D minor and C minor concertos (K466 and K491), in which, following an orchestral *decrescendo*, the first solo statement presents material not heard in the initial *tutti*. Here, slipping in with an improvisational, bluesy theme, the piano reclaims the F-sharp tonality first heard as a dissonant tingle against the G major arpeggios of the opening. The languorous E-major second subject, with its unabashed echoes of Tin Pan Alley, gives way to an exuberant toccata spiked with off-beat accents, fulfilling the dual roles of closing subject and development. In the recapitulation, the transition to the second subject becomes an extended harp solo while the subject itself is recast as the cadenza, the melody realized in a series of trills that recall Chopin's late B major Nocturne, op. 62 no. 1.

When asked to identify the most perilous passage of the Concerto in G, most pianists will unhesitatingly opt for the opening of the slow movement. Outwardly straightforward, it is utterly exposed, a compositional as well as pianistic tightrope. Ravel claimed the Adagio of Mozart's Clarinet Quintet as his model, reflecting that 'I compelled myself to *write* as well as I possibly could.' The Finale he described as 'a light movement in rondo form, conceived according to the strictest parameters'.[37] While the outlines of a Mozartian sonata-rondo are clearly discernible, equally crucial is a simple binary division, marked by the reprise of the opening material in the bassoons at bar 154 (fig. 14) – the exact midpoint of the 306-bar movement. Here, above the quicksilver semiquavers, fragments of the episodes jostle one another in what Roy Howat terms a sustained 'structural crescendo'.[38] Howat draws a parallel with Chabrier's *España*; we might recognize a similar template in Chopin's Third Ballade, which similarly fuses development and recapitulation, interweaving earlier motivic material over an inexorably rising bass ostinato. Typically Ravelian, though, is the four-bar fanfare that opens and closes the movement. That bookending – a characteristic gesture, evident also in *Sainte*,

Jeux d'eau, the 'Rigaudon' from *Le Tombeau de Couperin*, and the beginning and end of *L'Enfant et les sortilèges* – surely underlines the precise midpoint division.

The premiere of the Concerto in G, which took place on 14 January 1932, was followed immediately by what remained of Ravel's projected 'world tour'. While Manuel Rosenthal recalled that Ravel, travelling under Long's forceful wing, 'spoke rather like a little boy upon whom a governess has been imposed',[39] Long's own account does suggest that anyone touring with the composer needed all the patience, logistical mastery and sense of humour of a duenna:

> Every journey, the same scenes played out: he lost his luggage, his watch, his railway ticket or mine; kept his correspondence in his pocket, and mine too, which led to some awkward misadventures. 'We're making memories,' I would say to him, and we would laugh together. Our departures were indescribable: I wonder how we ever managed to catch a train. I would find him drowning in a sea of scores, photos that he never managed to sign, all his possessions scattered, encumbered by honours, ribbons, programmes that he insisted on bringing home for his dear brother Édouard.[40]

On the train to Vienna they realized that Ravel's precious concert shoes had been left in Paris; unconvinced by Long's assurance that a new pair could be bought in Austria, he ensured that they followed on the next train in the care of the engineer. In Romania an invitation to lunch with royalty went astray, leaving the king himself to telephone their hotel in search of them; in Poland a similar oversight almost prompted an international incident (relations between Poland and France then being tense), which took some careful diplomacy to smooth over.

It was on the Viennese leg of their tour, in the first week of February, that Ravel and Long first heard Wittgenstein play the Concerto for Left Hand, in a private performance (on two pianos) given after a celebratory dinner. Long recalled that over dinner she had listened, with a sinking feeling, as Wittgenstein explained to her that he had made 'some adjustments' to the work, the premiere of which he had given with the Vienna Philharmonic on 5 January. 'As he played,' she wrote, 'I followed the concerto, which I did not yet know, from the score, and could recognize in Ravel's ever-darkening face the damage caused by our host's initiatives.'[41] A forthright exchange of views followed, leaving Ravel so furious that he sent away the car that had come to fetch him and Long, and insisted on walking back to their hotel, the icy streets cooling his fury only a little.

Wittgenstein would reiterate his position in a subsequent, highly inflammatory letter. His modifications were not to the musical 'substance' but 'merely the instrumentation' of the Concerto (one can only imagine how the orchestrator of *Boléro* felt about that); they were of no importance, since Ravel would presumably be rewriting the work for two hands ('who will be playing a concerto for the left hand except me?'); and he would under no circumstances commit to playing it 'precisely as it is written'. 'No artist could submit to such a provision,' he declared, for 'we pianists make changes, small or large, in every concerto we play.'[42] This unconciliating missive must have been overtaken by a series of telegrams, for by the time Ravel received it the Paris premiere – scheduled for 25 March – had already been cancelled. As Wittgenstein retained exclusive performing rights until 1937, however, a rescheduled performance did take place in January 1933, Ravel conducting his intractable soloist with the Orchestre symphonique de Paris. One wonders whether Wittgenstein dialled down his 'modifications' for the occasion; certainly Ravel, on the podium, would have ensured the orchestra was working from *his* score. That Wittgenstein otherwise persisted in them, however, is borne out by his 1936 recording with Bruno Walter and the Royal Concertgebouw Orchestra, which includes (inter alia) handfuls of additional arpeggios and octaves in the cadenza.

By the time of this delayed premiere Ravel was at work again after several months of painful hiatus. On 8 October 1932 he had been involved in a serious taxi collision in Paris. Flung against the windscreen, he suffered cuts to his face and head, and contusions on his chest; among the several papers that carried the accident on their front pages, at least one (*Le Matin*) reported that he was knocked unconscious. Already fragile, Ravel was profoundly shaken by this incident. On 6 January 1933 he wrote to Manuel de Falla that although his injuries were not serious, for a long period he had been unable to do anything but eat and sleep, and that he retained an 'animal terror' of taxis, using them only as a very last resort.[43]

But it was not just taxis that were frightening him. Since the late 1920s, Ravel's periods of lassitude had become more regular and more debilitating, and at the end of 1930 he was writing again of potential 'neurasthenia' and 'cerebral anaemia'.[44] His close friends had also begun to notice certain changes in his behaviour: an unaccustomed deliberation in certain familiar gestures, and some odd new tics. Ravel's writing, too, was starting to change, his calligraphy visibly more constrained and irregular, his erasures more frequent. In the summer of 1932, during a visit to Saint-Jean-de-Luz, this vague shadow had coalesced into something far darker. On one occasion Marie Gaudin's nephew, Edmond, found Ravel rummaging in his pockets, unable to find the words to say that he wanted to smoke but couldn't find his cigarettes. Another day, he was throwing pebbles into the sea and accidentally sent one straight into Marie's face. More concerning still, one afternoon the composer who had for decades delighted in sea bathing suddenly 'forgot' how to swim and had to be rescued.[45] And in the same week that he wrote to Falla, in January 1933, Ravel had found himself unexpectedly unable to compel his hand to copy out a *feuillet d'album* of the Concerto in G.

And yet Ravel was working again, in a state of mingled fear and relief – 'I'd despaired,' he wrote to Marie on 3 January.[46] Six months earlier he had been commissioned to produce a serenade, a heroic song and a comic song for a film adaptation of *Don Quixote*, which was to feature the great Russian bass Feodor Chaliapin in the title role. The contract, signed in June 1932, had committed Ravel to produce the three songs within the space of three months – a time frame that would have been difficult in the best of circumstances, and by 1932 was simply impossible. By mid-September he had washed his hands of the project, and the film went ahead with songs hastily supplied by Jacques Ibert instead.

In the hope of recouping some of his fee, however, or perhaps stung by this rare failure to fulfil a commission – although perennially late, Ravel did usually manage to get there in the end – *Don Quichotte à Dulcinée* stayed with him. By the end of 1932 he had returned to his songs, his inspiration lubricated by the dance rhythms and harmonic colours of his beloved Spain. His 'Chanson romanesque' adopts the alternating $\frac{3}{4}$ and $\frac{6}{8}$ metres of the *quajira*, while the central 'Chanson épique' nods to the Basque *zortzico* in its rocking quintuple measure, underpinned by an organum-like accompaniment with an emotional concentration that recalls *Ronsard à son âme*. 'Chanson à boire' is a lively *jota*, with a decided echo of *Rapsodie espagnole* in its spiralling trumpet figures. Ravel's compositional career thus drew to a close in a flurry of exuberant *espagnolade*, and the Don's unfettered toast 'to joy!'

Having signed off *Don Quichotte* in April 1933, Ravel spent the summer trying to kick-start a ballet, or pantomime, or something in between, on the tale of Ali Baba and the Forty Thieves, titled *Morgiane*. An interview that June promised that this 'machine' 'will be very Grand-Guignol: the blood will run from beginning to end.'[47] He was also hoping to begin a project he had been talking about since 1928, an operatic work on the story of Jeanne d'Arc. His libretto was to be drawn from Joseph Delteil's popular biography (1925), a peculiar potpourri of burlesque and bawdiness, surrealism, hagiography and occasionally lyrical prose-poetry. Intrigued by the different facets of Jeanne, as child, warrior, saint and symbol, Ravel contemplated having two or even three performers in the role, and got as far as wondering how to craft the final scene – which was to depict Jeanne's arrival in Heaven – without actually bringing God on to the stage.[48] But not a note had yet been written, and by then it was too late.

In August 1933 Ravel wrote to Marie Gaudin, 'You won't see me at Saint-Jean this year, alas! I've been pretty wrecked for a long time, but am nevertheless continuing to work, without result as yet.'[49] Feeling 'more and more woozy', he had undergone a series

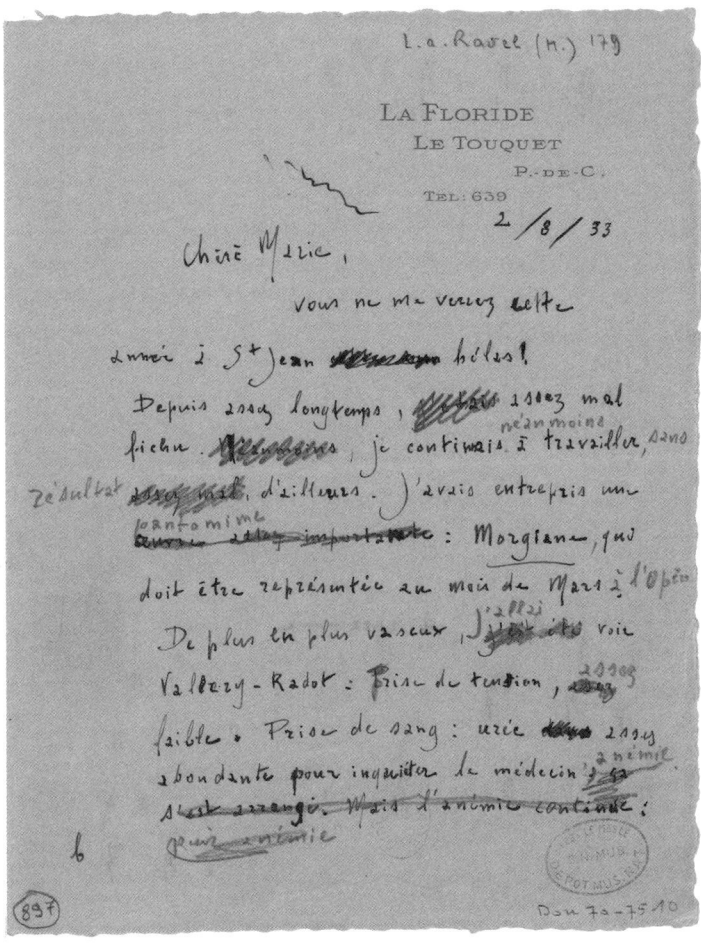

The painfully awkward draft of a letter to Marie Gaudin, 2 August 1933.

of examinations and had again been prescribed absolute rest, in the cooler north of France. Staying with his friends Jacques and Françoise Meyer in Le Touquet, he reported that he was feeling a little better. But any alleviation was illusory. On 19 November Ravel gave his last public performance, conducting *Boléro* and the Concerto in G at the Concerts Pasdeloup. A fortnight later he confirmed his regretful resignation from the Conseil supérieur of the Conservatoire. He was able to orchestrate *Don Quichotte à Dulcinée*, assisted by Rosenthal, and in November 1934 he would oversee Martial Singher's recording of the songs. (Although Rosenthal claimed to have orchestrated *Don Quichotte* under the composer's guidance, Roger Nichols asserts that the orchestral score is in Ravel's hand.[50]) Apart from some fragmentary sketches for *Morgiane*, and a few coaching sessions with performers (notably Jacques Février, who worked with him on the Concerto for Left Hand in March and October 1937), these were Ravel's last musical and professional acts.

On 30 January 1934 Ravel's physician Louis Pasteur Vallery-Radot wrote to Jourdan-Morhange:

> If you see Maurice Ravel's brother, tell him (without frightening him too much, for he seems to me to be extremely emotional) that I'm very anxious about his brother. I have conducted numerous examinations to be confident of not missing a lesion of some kind: there are none, but he is in a state of such anguished intellectual fatigue. He absolutely must rest completely for a long period – insist on this to Maurice Ravel.[51]

And from February until April Ravel did rest, first in a Swiss clinic, then in another in the western suburbs of Paris. By this time, however, anxiety had turned to grim despair, for no amount of repose or treatment was ameliorating the symptoms that were becoming inexorably and terrifyingly more acute. A brief note of sympathy to Maurice Delage, sent from Vevey, would arrive a full two weeks after the death of Delage's mother, a seeming lapse of courtesy that puzzled the Delages until Ravel explained that it had taken 'eight days to write, with the aid of the Larousse [dictionary]'.[52] He soon found himself unable even to sign autographs, and had to walk past hordes of mostly youthful admirers after concerts with an abruptness and seeming disdain that concealed – in Jourdan-Morhange's words – a heart 'bursting with bitterness'.[53]

A 2023 study of Ravel's medical history concludes that his symptoms, which manifested most obviously as aphasia (damage to the language centres in the brain), apraxia (loss of capacity to execute small movements) and agraphia (difficulty writing), point to a rare form of dementia called Logopenic Progressive Aphasia (LPA).[54] A subcategory of Primary Progressive Aphasia, LPA is caused by atrophy and the build-up of abnormal proteins around the left temporoparietal cortex, a region of the brain prominently involved in controlling speech and language, as well as limb movements. In his late fifties, his cognition and musical thought unimpaired, Ravel had thus been stricken by a degenerative disease that was remorselessly stripping him of his dignity, his capacity to communicate, his métier and his sense of self: if he could no longer compose, what would be left? To one friend he would insist, 'I've still *so much* to say in music, my head is full of it, alas, I cannot get my ideas onto paper!'[55] Long recalled him lamenting, 'I've written nothing, I'll leave nothing, I've said nothing of what I wanted to express!'[56] And Jourdan-Morhange left a heartbreaking description of Ravel weeping at a performance of *Daphnis*: 'I will never be able to write like that again [. . .] but it was good, all the same, it was good.'[57]

In February 1935, as a sixtieth birthday gift (and doubtless in the faint hope of stimulating *Morgiane*, which she had commissioned), Ida Rubinstein organized for Ravel to travel to Morocco and Spain in the care of the sculptor Léon Leyritz. The trip was intended to be as magical as possible: Ravel attended a magnificent wedding procession, travelled to a fortress high in the Atlas Mountains for a festival staged in his honour by a local noble, and was thrilled to see a snake-charmer. He was particularly delighted by a grand dinner in Fez at which there were 'more cats than men', completely in his element with one cat on his knees, another in his arms, a third draped around his shoulders and half a dozen more curling around his feet.[58] To Nelly Delage, Leyritz wrote on 6 March:

> despite the busyness here there is a sense of peace, an astonishing calm that is certainly beneficial. Combing was suddenly easy, and the buttons on his cuffs fastened themselves

by magic. The result of all this is that *he is in the middle of writing to his brother!* All alone! Slowly, of course, but it's true!

Three days later he exulted, '[Ravel] is speaking to me frequently about his music, no longer as if it were something unattainable [. . .] but as a *possible* thing, difficult, but possible. He has whistled to me tunes for *Morgiane* and spoken of the staging that he'd like to see.'[59] And Ravel indeed managed to write three sentences, including a brief description of lunch with a local notable: 'a feast worthy of a Thousand and One Nights. Only as one must eat with the fingers, I barely kept half of it.'[60] Those few laborious words of draft are followed by six attempts at a signature and some dogged, awkward practice at copying out the letters of the alphabet; the letter went unsent. Apart from a single-sentence fragment a few days later, this was probably the last letter Ravel tried to write himself. Thereafter, correspondence sent in his name would be written in other hands. No more was to be heard of *Morgiane*.

Trapped, desolate and tragically cognizant of his condition, in his last years Ravel withdrew from the world. A small, close-knit circle of friends cared for him devotedly: Jourdan-Morhange and Rosenthal, Roland-Manuel and the Meyers, and Jacques de Zogheb, a Montfort friend and neighbour who would drop in to sit with him every evening. Lucien Garban tended to his affairs at Durand, while the Delages kept a bedroom for him and assisted him with quiet, affectionate tact. It was Édouard, however, who remained Ravel's greatest source of comfort, and he would wait for 'hours' by the telephone for fear of missing a message from his brother. '"Do you think he'll come today?" he'd ask anxiously [. . .] and when Édouard did come [. . .] he could still be joyous,' Jourdan-Morhange recalled.[61] Otherwise, he mostly sat on his balcony, gaunt and silent. 'He seemed as if he might dissolve into nothing between one moment and the next,' wrote Colette.[62]

After 1935 Ravel's care was managed by the neurologists Thierry de Martel and Théophile Alajouanine. He submitted to many rounds of hospital stays, examinations and therapeutic interventions – electric shock treatment, speech therapy, injections, even hypnosis. In the autumn of 1937 he was examined by another neurosurgeon, Clovis Vincent, who offered a new hypothesis and a radical treatment. One hemisphere of the brain, Vincent suggested, had been 'depressed', possibly as a result of congenital hydrocephalus (given Ravel's small size and proportionately large head), and partly through the effects of tobacco, alcohol, trauma (the taxi accident) and age. Vincent proposed surgically 'reinflating' the hemisphere. The procedure, he stressed, had only 'a chance in a million' of success, and were Ravel 'some obscure Mr Smith' it would not be worth attempting. In this exceptional case, however, the potential benefits of a cure might equal the risks – and doing nothing would ensure that the degeneration would continue.[63]

Although Martel and Alajouanine were firmly opposed to surgical intervention, that infinitesimal possibility tipped the balance. Supported by a 'committee' comprised of Rosenthal, Delage and Roland-Manuel, Édouard Ravel gave Vincent permission to operate. Ravel himself was not consulted, his lack of agency doubtless reflecting his deterioration, as well as his friends' well-meaning desire to shield him from anxiety. Rosenthal, however, remembered

Coaching Jacques Février in the Concerto for Left Hand, October 1937.

him having his head shaved before the surgery; despite being falsely reassured that it was merely for another examination, Ravel replied calmly, 'I know they're going to slice my head' (*couper la cabèche*).⁶⁴

The operation took place on 17 December 1937. Vincent attempted unsuccessfully to inject the right lateral ventricle of the brain with water; his surgical notes say that it was 'collapsed' or 'sunken', but no haematoma or tumour was present.⁶⁵ Following the operation, Ravel seemingly recovered at least partial consciousness and was able to speak a little, but by 19 December he had slipped into a coma. He never awakened. At 3:30 a.m. on Tuesday, 28 December Ravel died in hospital, with Maurice Delage alone at his bedside.

Two days later Ravel was buried alongside his parents in the cemetery of Levallois-Perret. There was – of all things – an undertakers' strike, and it took the personal intervention of the Minister for Education and the Arts, Jean Zay, to procure a suitable casket. The funeral oration was given by Zay; among the mourners were Ravel's Conservatoire classmates and friends, Stravinsky and members of Les Six, as well as Ravel's beloved Basque cousins Marie Gaudin and Jane Courteault (*née* Gaudin). A tiny clip of Pathé news footage, viewable on YouTube, shows the cortège and some of the mourners, led by a sobbing Édouard.

Ravel's passing was marked in Paris and beyond with concerts and radio broadcasts, obituaries and tributes beyond number. Over and over again, the composer – Swiss-French on one side, so proudly Basque on the other – would be cast as the embodiment not just of contemporary French music but of French genius *in toto*. 'Almost no musician is as French as Ravel,' wrote Guy de Pourtalès at the start of the special 'Hommage à Ravel' issue of *La Revue musicale* in 1938, while Alfred Cortot declared that, just as Goethe had selected Rameau as his singular representative of French artistry, so would Ravel have been awarded the twentieth-century palm.⁶⁶

And indeed Ravel's oeuvre, spanning four decades of profound cultural and political transformation, was inextricably intertwined with the great artistic touchstones of his age: tradition and innovation in the wake of Wagner and Debussy; historiography and national identity; the dialogues between and across the creative arts.

The consistency of his artistic preoccupations, and his capacity to bind the past to the present, is perhaps epitomized in the common source that underpins his first orchestral work – the *Shéhérazade* overture – and the last, unrealized *Morgiane*. 'Exotic' tales-within-a-tale, prismatically translated by an eighteenth-century Frenchman, Antoine Galland's *Mille et une nuits* are a celebration not just of the power of storytelling but of the craft of the teller. 'I like to tell adventures in music!', Ravel told a Danish interviewer in 1926.[67] Through homage and pastiche, and through utterly serious interrogations of artistic purpose and principle, through the conversations he provoked and the histories he conjured, Ravel helped to furnish French music with a story it could tell about itself.

'For me, there are not several arts, but one alone,' Ravel wrote in 1931. 'Music, painting and literature differ only in their means of expression.'[68] Through his repeated emphasis on the translation of one art into another, he explicitly placed his own art within the greater adventure of French creative endeavour. He was a composer who worked at the borderlines, probing the porous grounds between expression and form, modernity and nostalgia, cool, mechanical irony and visceral emotion, and – murkiest of all – the artist's self and work. 'Since we cannot express ourselves without exploiting and thus transforming our emotions,' he mused, 'would it not be better at least to be fully aware [*conscient*], and to acknowledge that art is the supreme imposture? What is sometimes called my lack of sensibility is simply a scruple not to write just anything.'[69] *Conscience* – awareness, or self-knowledge – did ultimately entail an integration of the intellect and the spirit, intrinsic to a métier that demanded all one had to give. Thus, Ravel concluded simply and uncompromisingly in an addendum to the 'Autobiographical Sketch' of 1928, 'My object [. . .] is technical perfection. I can strive unceasingly towards this end, as I am certain that I will never attain it. The important thing is to get closer all the time.'[70]

References

Note on sources and abbreviations

This study is particularly indebted to the documentary scholarship of Arbie Orenstein, Roger Nichols and Manuel Cornejo. Orenstein's *A Ravel Reader* (OR), Nichols's landmark biography (NR) and Cornejo's monumental edition of Ravel's correspondence and writings (RI) were all indispensable sources. All citations of Ravel's correspondence come from Cornejo's collection; unless otherwise acknowledged, all translations are my own.

Among the wealth of contemporaneous memoirs, biographical studies and criticism, I draw particularly on the writings of Michel-Dmitri Calvocoressi and Roland-Manuel (notably the 1938 French and 1947 English editions of the latter's biography: RM38 and RM47 respectively); Hélène Jourdan-Morhange's *Ravel et nous* (JM); the special issue of *La Revue musicale* published to mark the first anniversary of Ravel's death in December 1938; and the 1939 collection *Maurice Ravel par quelques-uns de ses familiers* (RQF), together with the later memoirs of Manuel Rosenthal, as recorded by Marcel Marnat (MRos). Other primary source material is drawn predominantly from Gallica, the digital repository of the Bibliothèque nationale de France (www.gallica.fr), and the performance and criticism archive *Dezède* (www.dezede.org), together with the many volumes of the *Cahiers Maurice Ravel* (CMR).

There is a wealth of contemporary English-language scholarship on Ravel's life and work. Those interested in delving further are invited to explore the writings of Jessie Fillerup, Roy Howat, Steven Huebner, Peter Kaminsky, Barbara Kelly, Deborah Mawer, Michael Puri and Stephen Zank, together with the sources cited in the Bibliography.

Abbreviations

CMR *Cahiers Maurice Ravel* (1985–)
JM Hélène Jourdan-Morhange, *Ravel et nous* (Geneva, 1945)
MROS Marcel Marnat, ed., *Maurice Ravel: Souvenirs de Manuel Rosenthal* (Paris, 1995)
NR Roger Nichols, *Ravel* (New Haven, CT, and London, 2011)
OR Arbie Orenstein, ed., *A Ravel Reader: Correspondence, Articles, Interviews* (New York, 1990)
RI Manuel Cornejo, ed., *Maurice Ravel: L'Intégrale: Correspondance (1895–1937), écrits et entretiens* (Paris, 2018)
RM38; *RM47* Roland-Manuel, *À la gloire de Ravel* (Paris, 1938); English edition: *Maurice Ravel*, trans. Cynthia Jolly (London, 1947)
RQF Émile Vuillermoz et al., *Maurice Ravel par quelques-uns de ses familiers* (Paris, 1939)

Preface

1 Jacques de Zogheb, 'Souvenirs raveliens', in *RQF*, p. 172.
2 Michel-Dmitri Calvocoressi, 'Maurice Ravel', *Musical Times*, LIV/850 (December 1913), p. 785.
3 Michel-Dmitri Calvocoressi, *Musicians' Gallery* (London, 1933), p. 51. See also Roland-Manuel, 'Maurice Ravel ou l'esthétique de l'imposture', *La Revue musicale*, VI/6 ('Maurice Ravel', April 1925), pp. 16–21.
4 Michel-Dmitri Calvocoressi, 'When Ravel Composed to Order', *Music & Letters*, XXII/1 (January 1941), p. 54. See also Steven Huebner, 'Maurice Ravel: Private Life, Public Works', in *Musical Biography: Towards New Paradigms*, ed. Jolanta T. Pekacz (Abingdon and New York, 2006), pp. 69–88; and Barbara L. Kelly, 'Re-Presenting Ravel: Artificiality and the Aesthetic of Imposture', in *Unmasking Ravel: New Perspectives on the Music*, ed. Peter Kaminsky (Rochester, NY, 2011), pp. 41–62.
5 Calvocoressi, *Musicians' Gallery*, p. 52.
6 See Roger Nichols, *From Berlioz to Boulez* (London, 2022), pp. 189–201.
7 Roger Nichols, ed., *Ravel Remembered* (London, 1987), p. 63.
8 *New York Times*, 7 August 1927 (*OR*, p. 450); *RI*, p. 1424.
9 *RI*, p. 129.
10 René Chalupt, 'Maurice Ravel et les prétextes littéraires de sa musique', *La Revue musicale*, VI/6 ('Maurice Ravel', April 1925), p. 65.
11 *ABC de Madrid*, 1 May 1924 (*OR*, p. 433); *NR*, p. 87.

12 Léon-Paul Fargue, *Maurice Ravel* (Paris, 1949), p. 29.
13 Madeleine Goss, *Bolero: The Life of Maurice Ravel* (New York, 1940), p. 221; Charles Alvar Harding, 'Maurice Ravel Away from His Music', *Musical Courier*, 20 May 1933.
14 *RI*, p. 674 (letter of 15 January 1920).
15 *MROS*, p. 128.
16 Michel-Dmitri Calvocoressi, 'Maurice Ravel, 1875–1937', *Musical Times*, LXXIX/1139 (January 1938), p. 23.
17 Goss, *Bolero*, p. 21.
18 Calvocoressi, 'Maurice Ravel, 1875–1937', p. 23; *RM47*, p. 129.
19 Fargue, *Maurice Ravel*, p. 7.
20 *New York Times*, 26 February 1928; *OR*, p. 456.
21 *MROS*, pp. 120–21.
22 René Chalupt and Marcelle Gerar, *Ravel au miroir de ses lettres* (Paris, 1956), p. 241.
23 *RI*, p. 612. My emphasis.
24 *MROS*, p. 183.
25 Fargue, *Maurice Ravel*, p. 59.
26 *RI*, p. 65.
27 See Roger Nichols, 'La Sexualité de Maurice Ravel', *CMR*, XVI (2013–14), pp. 125–8.
28 *RI*, p. 172.

1 The Engineer, the Basque and the Dandy

1 Pierre Souvestre, 'Les Précurseurs: Joseph Ravel', *L'Auto-vélo*, 17 October 1908.
2 *RI*, p. 838.
3 *New York Times*, 7 August 1927; *OR*, p. 450.
4 Jacques de Zogheb, 'Souvenirs raveliens', in *RQF*, p. 172.
5 *RI*, pp. 88 and 697.
6 'Mes souvenirs d'enfant paresseux', *La Petite Gironde*, 12 July 1931; *RI*, p. 1443.
7 *NR*, p. 9.
8 'Mes souvenirs d'enfant paresseux'; *RI*, p. 1443.
9 Nina Gubisch, 'La Vie musicale à Paris entre 1887 et 1914 à travers le journal de R. Viñes', *Revue internationale de musique française*, 1/2 (June 1980), p. 179.
10 *RI*, p. 1633.

11 Ibid., pp. 1634–5.
12 Gubisch, 'Le journal de R. Viñes', p. 184.
13 'Quand Ravel scandalisait son professeur d'harmonie', *Paris-Soir*, 28 December 1937. The article also suggests that he brought Satie's *Sarabandes* to Pessard, but this seems less likely (they were then unpublished).
14 *RI*, p. 1224.
15 Nina Gubisch, 'Les Années de jeunesse d'un pianiste espagnol en France (1887–1900): Journal et correspondance de Ricardo Viñes', diss., Paris Conservatoire, 1971, p. 141.
16 Jean Françaix, *De La Musique et des musiciens* (Paris, 1999), pp. 171–2.
17 Madeleine Goss, *Bolero: The Life of Maurice Ravel* (New York, 1940), p. 34.
18 Gubisch, 'Le journal de R. Viñes', pp. 190–91.
19 Ibid., p. 188.
20 Roy Howat, *The Art of French Piano Music: Debussy, Ravel, Fauré, Chabrier* (New Haven, CT, and London, 2009), p. 145.
21 Gubisch, 'Le journal de R. Viñes', pp. 183 and 186.
22 'Mes souvenirs d'enfant paresseux'; *RI*, p. 1443.
23 Charles Baudelaire, 'Salon de 1846', in *Œuvres complètes*, vol. II, ed. Claude Pichois (Paris, 1976), p. 432.
24 'Mes souvenirs d'enfant paresseux'; *RI*, p. 1444.
25 *JM*, p. 134.
26 Heath Lees, *Mallarmé and Wagner: Music and Poetic Language* (Aldershot, 2007), p. 136.
27 Ibid., pp. 131 and xv–xvi.
28 *RI*, p. 157.
29 Ibid., p. 1055.
30 Arbie Orenstein, *Ravel: Man and Musician* (New York, 1975, revd edn 1991), p. 145.
31 Gubisch, 'Le journal de R. Viñes', p. 194.
32 *Le guide musical*, 13 March 1898; *Le progrès artistique*, 10 March 1898.
33 Nina Gubisch, 'Ravel, Viñes, les années de formation: Goûts croisés, curiosités partagées', *CMR*, XIV (2011), p. 32.
34 Charles Koechlin, *Gabriel Fauré* (Paris, 1949), p. 17.
35 *RI*, p. 1636.
36 *RM38*, p. 40.
37 Ibid., pp. 40–41.
38 Marguerite de Saint-Marceaux, *Journal, 1894–1927*, ed. Myriam Chimènes (Paris, 2007), pp. 171–3.
39 *RI*, p. 66.

40 Colette, 'Un salon en 1900', in *RQF*, pp. 119–20.
41 Tristan Klingsor, 'L'Époque Ravel', in *RQF*, p. 125.
42 Colette, 'Un salon', p. 119.
43 Klingsor, 'L'Époque Ravel', p. 125.
44 Gubisch, 'Le journal de R. Viñes', p. 195.
45 Ibid., p. 197.
46 *L'Écho de Paris*, 30 May 1899.
47 *RM38*, p. 44.
48 *RI*, pp. 70–71.
49 *L'Écho de Paris*, 30 January 1900.
50 *RI*, p. 72.
51 Charles Oulmont, 'Souvenir', *La Revue musicale*, XIX/187 ('Hommage à Ravel', December 1938), p. 209.
52 *RI*, pp. 74–6.
53 *Berlingske Tidende*, 30 January 1926 (*RI*, p. 1502); *RM47*, p. 29.

2 *Agent provocateur*

1 Marguerite de Saint-Marceaux, *Journal, 1894–1927*, ed. Myriam Chimènes (Paris, 2007), p. 276.
2 *RI*, pp. 74–5.
3 *JM*, p. 90.
4 *Le Temps*, 22 April 1902.
5 *RI*, p. 72.
6 Paul Ladmirault, 'Ravel', *La Revue musicale*, XIX/187 ('Hommage à Ravel', December 1938), p. 214.
7 *La Revue musicale*, IV/6 (15 March 1904) and IV/8 (15 April 1904).
8 *Le Temps*, 19 April 1904.
9 *Mercure de France*, L/174 (1 April 1904), pp. 250–51.
10 Ravel's great-aunt Gracieuse Billac ('Gachoucha') was for six decades a household servant to the Gaudin family in Saint-Jean-de-Luz. Ravel – born in the servants' quarters of their Ciboure home – considered the Gaudins his cousins, being particularly close to Jane and her sister Marie. *NR*, p. 7; *RI*, p. 77n; Étienne Rousseau-Plotto, *Ravel: portraits basques* (Anglet, 2004), pp. 52–4.
11 *RI*, p. 87.
12 Jann Pasler, 'A Sociology of the Apaches: "Sacred Battalion" for *Pelléas*', in *Berlioz and Debussy: Sources, Contexts and Legacies*, ed. Barbara Kelly and Kerry Murphy (Aldershot, 2007), p. 155.

13 Maurice Delage, 'Les Premiers Amis de Ravel', in *RQF*, p. 99.
14 Malou Haine, 'Cipa Godebski et les Apaches', *Revue belge de musicologie*, LX (2006), pp. 237–8.
15 Léon-Paul Fargue, *Maurice Ravel* (Paris, 1949), p. 57.
16 Ibid., p. 53.
17 Pasler, 'A Sociology', p. 157.
18 Émile Vuillermoz, 'L'Œuvre de Maurice Ravel', in *RQF*, p. 66.
19 Pasler, 'A Sociology', p. 157.
20 Tristan Klingsor, 'L'Époque Ravel', in *RQF*, p. 128.
21 Nina Gubisch, 'La Vie musicale à Paris entre 1887 et 1914 à travers le journal de R. Viñes', *Revue internationale de musique française*, 1/2 (June 1980), p. 203.
22 Arbie Orenstein, *Ravel, Man and Musician* (New York, 1975), p. 160; *RI*, pp. 105–6.
23 Delage, 'Les Premiers Amis', p. 103.
24 Vuillermoz, 'L'Œuvre', p. 31.
25 Paul Roberts, *Reflections: The Piano Music of Maurice Ravel* (Milwaukee, WI, 2012), pp. 57–62.
26 Ibid., p. 51.
27 Fargue, *Maurice Ravel*, p. 57.
28 *RI*, p. 96.
29 Ibid., p. 98.
30 *Le Mercure musical*, 1/1 (15 May 1905), p. 46.
31 Ibid., p. 100.
32 *NR*, pp. 64–5.
33 *RI*, p. 104.
34 Delage, 'Les Premiers Amis', p. 105.
35 *RI*, pp. 102, 104 and 106.
36 Ibid., p. 108.
37 Charles Baudelaire, 'Salon de 1859', in *Œuvres complètes*, vol. II, ed. Claude Pichois (Paris, 1976), p. 741.
38 *RI*, pp. 115–16.
39 Paul Watt, 'Musical and Literary Networks in the *Weekly Critical Review*, Paris, 1903–1904', *Nineteenth-Century Music Review*, XIV/1 (April 2017), p. 40.
40 *RI*, p. 114.
41 Jacques Durand, *Quelques souvenirs d'un éditeur de musique*, vol. I (Paris, 1925), p. 132.
42 René Dumesnil, 'Maurice Ravel poète', *La Revue musicale*, XIX/187 ('Hommage à Maurice Ravel', December 1938), p. 126.
43 *Mercure musical*, II/3 (1 February 1906), p. 121.

44 *Le Temps*, 30 January 1906.
45 *RI*, p. 127.
46 See Emily Kilpatrick, *French Art Song: History of a New Music* (Rochester, NY, 2022), pp. 274–80.
47 *RI*, p. 126.
48 Ibid., p. 128.
49 Ibid., pp. 137 and 144.
50 Fernand Divoire et al., 'Sous la Musique que faut-il mettre?', *Musica*, 102 (March 1911), p. 59; *RI*, p. 1457.
51 Malou Haine, 'Cinq entretiens inédits de Jane Bathori avec Stéphane Audel', *Revue musicale de Suisse romande*, LXI/2 (June 2008), p. 25.
52 *Le Courrier musical*, 1 February 1907, p. 78.
53 *NR*, p. 89.
54 *RI*, p. 156.
55 See Kilpatrick, *French Art Song*, pp. 241–5.

3 Dances with History

1 *RI*, p. 157.
2 Ibid., pp. 166 and 143.
3 Émile Vuillermoz, 'Les Théâtres: *L'Heure espagnole*', *Revue musicale SIM*, VII/6 (15 June 1911), p. 67.
4 *RI*, pp. 160, 162 and 173.
5 *Comœdia*, 11 May 1911; *RI*, p. 1459.
6 Richard Langham Smith, 'Ravel's Operatic Spectacles: *L'Heure* and *L'Enfant*', in *The Cambridge Companion to Ravel*, ed. Deborah Mawer (Cambridge, 2000), p. 199.
7 *L'Intransigeant*, 17 May 1911; *RI*, p. 1460.
8 *L'Action française*, 22 May 1911.
9 *RI*, p. 176.
10 Manuel de Falla, *On Music and Musicians*, ed. Federico Sopeña, trans. D. Urman and J. M. Thomson (London and Boston, MA, 1979), p. 94.
11 Marguerite de Saint-Marceaux, *Journal, 1894–1927*, ed. Myriam Chimènes (Paris, 2007), p. 326.
12 Ralph Vaughan Williams, 'A Musical Autobiography', in *National Music and Other Essays* (Oxford, 1963), p. 191.
13 Steven Baur, 'Ravel's "Russian" Period: Octatonicism in His Early Works, 1893–1908', *Journal of the American Musicological Society*, LII/3 (Autumn 1999), pp. 569–76.

14 *RI*, p. 179.
15 Ibid., pp. 181 and 187–8.
16 René Chalupt, 'Maurice Ravel et les prétextes littéraires de sa musique', *La Revue musicale*, VI/6 ('Maurice Ravel', April 1925), p. 67.
17 Roy Howat, *The Art of French Piano Music: Debussy, Ravel, Fauré, Chabrier* (New Haven, CT, and London, 2009), pp. 47–9.
18 *RI*, p. 193.
19 Quoted in Roger Nichols, ed., *Ravel Remembered* (London, 1987), p. 19.
20 *JM*, p. 189.
21 *RI*, pp. 206 and 219.
22 Ibid., p. 206.
23 Ibid., p. 68.
24 Barbara Kelly, *Music and Ultramodernism in France: A Fragile Consensus, 1913–1939* (Woodbridge, 2013), p. 39.
25 *RI*, p. 304.
26 Ibid., pp. 252 and 256.
27 See Michael Puri, 'Ravel's *Valses nobles et sentimentales* and Its Models', *Music Theory Online*, XXIII/3 (2017).
28 *Le Temps*, 28 May 1911; *Revue des deux mondes*, VI/4 (1 July 1911), pp. 218–19.
29 *Revue musicale SIM*, VII/6 (15 June 1911), p. 67; *Mercure de France*, XCI/336 (16 June 1911), pp. 869–70.
30 *Le Figaro*, 20 May 1911; see Emily Kilpatrick, *The Operas of Maurice Ravel* (Cambridge, 2015), pp. 26–32.
31 *RI*, p. 214.
32 Michel Fokine, *Memoirs of a Ballet Master*, trans. Vitale Fokine (London, 1961), p. 196. See Simon Morrison, 'The Origins of *Daphnis et Chloé* (1912)', *19th-Century Music*, XXVIII/1 (Summer 2004), p. 57.
33 *NR*, p. 143.
34 Ibid., p. 145.
35 *RI*, p. 285.
36 Ibid., pp. 294–5.
37 Jacques Durand, *Quelques souvenirs d'un éditeur de musique*, vol. II (Paris, 1925), p. 17; Fokine, *Memoirs*, p. 202.
38 *RI*, p. 670.
39 *Revue musicale SIM*, VIII/6 (15 June 1912), p. 67.
40 *RI*, p. 311.
41 Ibid., pp. 317–18 and 326.
42 Ibid., p. 310.
43 *NR*, p. 153.

44 *RI*, p. 320.
45 See Emily Kilpatrick, 'Ravel's *Trois poèmes de Stéphane Mallarmé*: A Philosophy of Composition', *Music & Letters*, CI/3 (2020), pp. 532–9.
46 Howat, *The Art of French Piano Music*, pp. 88–90.
47 On Ravel's musical criticism see Emily Kilpatrick, 'Maurice Ravel and the Poetics of Originality, 1907–14', *Music & Letters* (November 2024), published online at https://doi.org/10.1093/ml/gcae096.
48 *Comœdia illustré*, VI/8 (20 January 1914); *RI*, p. 1416.
49 *Revue musicale SIM*, VIII/3 and VIII/2 (15 March and 15 February 1912); *RI*, pp. 1383–5.
50 *Revue musicale SIM*, VIII/4 (15 April 1912); *Les Cahiers d'aujourd'hui*, February 1913; *RI*, pp. 1390 and 1401–2.
51 *Comœdia illustré*, V/8 (20 January 1913); *RI*, pp. 1395–6.
52 *Comœdia illustré*, V/7 (5 January 1913); *RI*, p. 1392.
53 *RI*, p. 316.

4 An Unknown Destination

1 *RI*, p. 351.
2 Roland-Manuel, *Maurice Ravel et son œuvre* (Paris, 1914), p. 39.
3 *RI*, pp. 356 and 358.
4 Ibid., p. 176.
5 See Arbie Orenstein, 'Some Unpublished Music and Letters by Maurice Ravel', *Music Forum*, III (1973), pp. 328–31; and Barbara Kelly, 'History and Homage', in *The Cambridge Companion to Ravel*, ed. Deborah Mawer (Cambridge, 2000), pp. 19–22.
6 *RI*, p. 376.
7 Ibid., pp. 382–3.
8 Ibid., p. 384.
9 Ibid., pp. 389–90 and 392.
10 Ibid., p. 396.
11 See Roy Howat, 'Le *Trio* de Ravel cent ans après', *CMR*, XVII (2014–15), pp. 70–78.
12 Théodore de Banville, *Petit Traité de poésie française* (Paris, 1872), p. 219.
13 Brian Newbould, 'Ravel's Pantoum', *Musical Times*, CXVI/1585 (March 1975), p. 228.
14 Jacques Durand, *Quelques souvenirs d'un éditeur de musique*, vol. II (Paris, 1925), p. 80.
15 *RI*, p. 402.

16 See Emily Kilpatrick, 'Into the Woods: Retelling the Wartime Fairytales of Maurice Ravel', *Musical Times*, CIL/1902 (Spring 2008), pp. 57–66.
17 *RI*, pp. 409–10.
18 Ibid., p. 423.
19 Ibid., pp. 425, 428 and 434–5.
20 Ibid., pp. 442–3.
21 Ibid., p. 446.
22 Ibid., pp. 452, 464 and 477.
23 Ibid., pp. 501 and 476.
24 Ibid., pp. 438 and 503.
25 Ibid., pp. 513, 482 and 509.
26 Ibid., pp. 486–7.
27 Ibid., p. 559.
28 Michel Duchesneau, *L'Avant-garde musicale et ses sociétés à Paris de 1871 à 1939* (Liège, 1997), p. 100.
29 *RI*, p. 267 (19 July 1911).
30 Marguerite de Saint-Marceaux, *Journal, 1894–1927*, ed. Myriam Chimènes (Paris, 2007), p. 926.
31 *RM38*, p. 133.
32 *RI*, p. 612.
33 *Le Rempart*, 4 June 1933; *RI*, p. 1571.
34 Marguerite Long, *Au Piano avec Maurice Ravel* (Paris, 1971), pp. 142–3.
35 Scott Messing, 'Polemic as History: The Case of Neoclassicism', *Journal of Musicology*, IX/4 (Autumn 1991), pp. 485–9; Paul Roberts, *Reflections: The Piano Music of Maurice Ravel* (Milwaukee, WI, 2012), p. 119.
36 Kelly, 'History and Homage', p. 20.
37 Rex Lawson, 'Maurice Ravel: *Frontispice* for Pianola', *Pianola Journal*, II (1989), pp. 35–8.
38 *RI*, pp. 598 and 602.
39 Ibid., p. 629.
40 Ibid., pp. 660–61, 665 and 683.
41 *MROS*, p. 72.
42 *Le Ménestrel*, 17 December 1920.
43 Deborah Mawer, 'Ballet and the Apotheosis of the Dance', in *The Cambridge Companion to Ravel*, ed. Mawer, pp. 153–4.
44 *De Telegraaf*, 30 September 1922; *RI*, p. 1478.
45 *RI*, p. 848.
46 Ibid., p. 1084.
47 Ibid., pp. 669 and 671.
48 *NR*, p. 207.

49 *RI*, p. 674.
50 *RM47*, p. 84 ('his continually repeated, Baudelairean horror of decorations').
51 *RI*, pp. 677 and 681.
52 *Le Coq*, 1 May 1920.
53 *RI*, p. 690.
54 Ibid., p. 142.
55 Ibid., p. 671.
56 Quoted in Roger Nichols, ed., *Ravel Remembered* (London, 1987), pp. 117–18.
57 *RI*, p. 724.
58 *NR*, p. 222.
59 'Wiener Eindrucke eines französischen Künstlers', *Neue Freie Presse*, 29 October 1920; *OR*, pp. 419–20.

5 The Compositional Machine

1 *RI*, pp. 714–15 and 699.
2 Ibid., pp. 688 and 731.
3 Marcel Marnat, *Maurice Ravel* (Paris, 1986), p. 498.
4 *JM*, p. 26.
5 Ibid., p. 24.
6 *RI*, p. 756.
7 Ibid., p. 805.
8 Ibid., p. 877.
9 Ibid., p. 979.
10 Ibid., p. 753.
11 *NR*, p. 225.
12 *RI*, p. 869.
13 *MROS*, pp. 37–8.
14 *RI*, p. 816.
15 'Mes souvenirs d'enfant paresseux', *La Petite Gironde*, 12 July 1931; *RI*, p. 1445.
16 *RI*, p. 799.
17 Barbara Kelly, *Music and Ultramodernism in France: A Fragile Consensus, 1913–1939* (Woodbridge, 2013), p. 83.
18 Ibid., p. 168; Paul Landormy, 'Le Déclin de l'impressionnisme', *La Revue musicale*, II/4 (February 1921), p. 109.
19 Roland-Manuel, 'Maurice Ravel', *La Revue musicale*, II/6 (April 1921), p. 17.

20 *RI*, pp. 873–4.
21 *JM*, p. 99.
22 *Le Courrier musical*, 24 November 1921.
23 *Berlingske Tidende*, 4 May 1924; *RI*, p. 1486.
24 *RI*, p. 974.
25 Roger Nichols, ed., *Ravel Remembered* (London, 1987), pp. 115–16.
26 *RI*, p. 805.
27 Roy Howat, *The Art of French Piano Music: Debussy, Ravel, Fauré, Chabrier* (New Haven, CT, and London, 2009), p. 321.
28 *RI*, p. 810.
29 Ibid., p. 850.
30 Ibid., pp. 868 and 881.
31 Ibid., p. 884.
32 Ibid., p. 1085.
33 Howat, *The Art of French Piano Music*, p. 321, n47.
34 *RI*, p. 891.
35 Nichols, ed., *Ravel Remembered*, p. 92.
36 Paul Stefan, 'Quelques souvenirs sur Ravel', *La Revue musicale*, XIX/187 ('Hommage à Maurice Ravel', December 1938), p. 278.
37 Gérard Zwang, *Mémoires d'une chanteuse française: La Vie et les amours de Madeleine Grey (1896–1979)* (Paris, 2008), pp. 111–12.
38 *De Telegraaf*, 30 September 1922; *OR*, p. 424.
39 *ABC de Madrid*, 1 May 1924; *OR*, p. 433.
40 *The Star*, 16 October 1923; *OR*, p. 428.
41 *RI*, p. 911.
42 *NR*, pp. 254–5.
43 *RI*, p. 934.
44 *NR*, p. 256.
45 *RI*, p. 950.
46 *JM*, p. 181; *RI*, p. 947.
47 Joseph MacLeod, *The Sisters d'Aranyi* (London, 1969), p. 147.
48 *RI*, p. 966.
49 Emily Kilpatrick, *The Operas of Maurice Ravel* (Cambridge, 2015), p. 64.
50 Ibid., p. 65; Roland-Manuel, *Maurice Ravel et son œuvre dramatique* (Paris, 1928), p. 93.
51 Colette, 'Un salon en 1900', in *RQF*, p. 121.
52 See Kilpatrick, *The Operas of Maurice Ravel*, pp. 38–44.
53 Colette, *Mes apprentissages*, in *Œuvres complètes*, vol. III, ed. Claude Pichois (Paris, 1991), p. 1069.

54 *JM*, p. 127.
55 Colette, *L'Étoile vesper*, in *Œuvres completes*, ed. Claude Pichois, vol. IV (Paris, 2001), p. 853; Maurice Goudeket, *Close to Colette*, trans. Enid McLeod (London, 1957), p. 112.
56 *RI*, p. 629.
57 Ibid., p. 631.
58 Ibid., pp. 714–15.
59 Ibid., p. 976.
60 Ibid., pp. 999–1000.
61 *JM*, p. 123.
62 Kilpatrick, *The Operas of Maurice Ravel*, p. 46.
63 Ibid., p. 47.
64 *RI*, p. 1058.
65 Claude Pichois, *Colette* (Paris, 1998), p. 285.
66 Kilpatrick, *The Operas of Maurice Ravel*, pp. 49–50.
67 *RI*, p. 1009.
68 *MROS*, p. 119.
69 *NR*, p. 274.
70 Ibid., p. 280.
71 *RI*, p. 1100.
72 Ibid., pp. 1112–13.
73 *NR*, p. 285.
74 *MROS*, p. 110.
75 Deborah Mawer, 'Crossing Borders II: Ravel's Theory and Practice of Jazz', in *Ravel Studies*, ed. Mawer (Cambridge, 2010), pp. 133–5.
76 *OR*, p. 46.
77 *RI*, p. 925.
78 *Berlingske Tidende*, 4 May 1924; *RI*, p. 1488.
79 'On Inspiration', *The Chesterian*, IX/68 (January–February 1928), p. 115; *OR*, p. 389.
80 *RI*, p. 951.
81 *Berlingske Tidende*, 4 May 1924; *RI*, p. 1486.
82 *OR*, p. 389, n3.

6 Dissolving

1 *RI*, p. 1148.
2 *NR*, p. 291.

3 *RI*, p. 1158. See also Nicholas Gebhardt, 'Crossing Borders 1: The Historical Context for Ravel's North American Tour', in *Ravel Studies*, ed. Deborah Mawer (Cambridge, 2010), pp. 92–113.
4 *RI*, pp. 1169, 1156–7 and 1164.
5 Ibid., pp. 1168 and 1160–61.
6 Ibid., p. 1172.
7 Joaquín Nin, 'Comment est né le *Boléro* de Ravel', *La Revue musicale*, XIX/187 ('Hommage à Maurice Ravel', December 1938), p. 212.
8 *RI*, p. 1185.
9 *Le Ménestrel*, 21 November 1930.
10 *NR*, p. 298.
11 *RI*, p. 1200.
12 *Evening Standard*, 24 February 1932; *OR*, p. 491.
13 *OR*, p. 328.
14 Jane Bathori, 'Les Musiciens que j'ai connus', trans. Felix Aprahamian, *Recorded Sound*, 1/5 (1961), p. 150; *Daily Telegraph*, 11 July 1931; *OR*, p. 477.
15 Marguerite Long, *Au Piano avec Maurice Ravel* (Paris, 1971), p. 171.
16 *Excelsior*, 30 October 1931; *RI*, p. 1557.
17 *Le Rempart*, 4 June 1933; *RI*, p. 1572.
18 Charles Alvar Harding, 'Maurice Ravel Away from His Music', *Musical Courier*, 20 May 1933; *NR*, p. 296.
19 See Deborah Mawer, *The Ballets of Maurice Ravel: Creation and Interpretation* (Aldershot, 2006), p. 212.
20 *RI*, p. 1213.
21 Ibid., p. 1225.
22 Ibid., p. 1227.
23 Ibid., p. 1237.
24 Ibid., p. 1243.
25 Ibid., p. 1248.
26 *JM*, p. 36.
27 *RI*, pp. 1256, 1260 and 1267.
28 Ibid., pp. 1266, 1272 and 1274.
29 Long, *Au Piano*, p. 89; see also Jessie Fillerup, *Magician of Sound: Ravel and the Aesthetics of Illusion* (Oakland, CA, 2021), pp. 117–20.
30 *Le Journal*, 14 January 1933; *RI*, p. 1446.
31 Ibid.
32 *Le Nouvelliste*, 25 April 1932; *RI*, p. 1567.
33 *Daily Telegraph*, 11 July 1931; *OR*, p. 477.
34 *Die Telegraaf*, 6 April 1932; *OR*, p. 493.

35 Andy Fry, 'La Guerre et la paix, 1914–1945', in *The Cambridge Companion to French Music*, ed. Simon Trezise (Cambridge, 2015), p. 169.
36 *Excelsior*, 30 October 1931; *RI*, p. 1557.
37 Ibid.
38 Roy Howat, *The Art of French Piano Music: Debussy, Ravel, Fauré, Chabrier* (New Haven, CT, and London, 2009), p. 47.
39 *MROS*, p. 51.
40 Long, *Au Piano*, pp. 63–4.
41 Ibid., p. 87.
42 *RI*, pp. 1281–2.
43 Ibid., p. 1301.
44 Ibid., p. 1262.
45 Étienne Rousseau-Plotto, *Ravel: Portraits basques* (Anglet, 2004), pp. 256–7.
46 *RI*, p. 1300.
47 *Le Rempart*, 4 June 1933; *RI*, p. 1572.
48 *JM*, p. 236.
49 *RI*, p. 1314.
50 *NR*, p. 334; *MROS*, pp. 180–81.
51 *RI*, p. 1320.
52 Ibid., p. 1322.
53 *JM*, p. 244.
54 Bernard Lechevalier, Bernard Mercier and Fausto Viader, *Le Cerveau de Ravel* (Paris, 2023), pp. 279 and 283; Maya L. Henry and Maria Luisa Gorno-Tempini, 'The Logopenic Variant of Primary Progressive Aphasia', *Current Opinion in Neurology*, XXIII/6 (December 2010), pp. 633–7.
55 *RI*, p. 1345.
56 Quoted in Long, *Au Piano*, p. 176.
57 *JM*, p. 240.
58 Ibid., p. 228.
59 *RI*, pp. 1329–30.
60 Ibid., p. 1329.
61 *JM*, p. 247.
62 Colette, 'Un salon en 1900', in *RQF*, p. 123.
63 *MROS*, pp. 188–9.
64 Ibid., p. 190.
65 Eric Baeck, 'The Longstanding Medical Fascination with "le cas Ravel"', in *Ravel Studies*, ed. Mawer, p. 200.
66 Guy de Poutalès, 'Petit Hommage à Ravel', and Alfred Cortot, 'Dans le souvenir de Maurice Ravel', *La Revue musicale*, XIX/187 ('Hommage à Ravel', December 1938), pp. 34 and 37.

67 *Berlingske Tidende*, 30 January 1926; OR, p. 440.
68 'Mes souvenirs d'enfant paresseux', *La Petite Gironde*, 12 July 1931; RI, p. 1443.
69 Ibid., RI, p. 1445.
70 'Quelques réflexions sur la musique', RI, p. 1442.

Bibliography

Bathori, Jane, 'Les Musiciens que j'ai connus', trans. Felix Aprahamian, *Recorded Sound*, I/5 (1961), pp. 144–51

Baur, Steven, 'Ravel's "Russian" Period: Octatonicism in His Early Works, 1893–1908', *Journal of the American Musicological Society*, LII/3 (Autumn 1999), pp. 531–92

Calvocoressi, Michel-Dmitri, 'Maurice Ravel', *Musical Times*, LIV/850 (December 1913), pp. 785–7

—, *Musicians' Gallery* (London, 1933)

—, 'Maurice Ravel, 1875–1937', *Musical Times*, LXXIX/1139 (January 1938), pp. 22–4

—, 'When Ravel Composed to Order', *Music & Letters*, XXII/1 (January 1941), pp. 54–9

Chalupt, René, and Marcelle Gerar, *Ravel au miroir de ses lettres* (Paris, 1956)

de Falla, Manuel, *On Music and Musicians*, ed. Federico Sopeña, trans. D. Urman and J. M. Thomson (London and Boston, MA, 1979)

Duchesneau, Michel, *L'Avant-garde musicale et ses sociétés à Paris de 1871 à 1939* (Liège, 1997)

Durand, Jacques, *Quelques souvenirs d'un éditeur de musique*, vol. I (Paris, 1925)

Fargue, Léon-Paul, *Maurice Ravel* (Paris, 1949)

Fillerup, Jessie, *Magician of Sound: Ravel and the Aesthetics of Illusion* (Oakland, CA, 2021)

Fokine, Michel, *Memoirs of a Ballet Master*, trans. Vitale Fokine (London, 1961)

Goss, Madeleine, *Bolero: The Life of Maurice Ravel* (New York, 1940)

Goudeket, Maurice, *Close to Colette*, trans. Enid McLeod (London, 1957)

Gubisch, Nina, 'La Vie musicale à Paris entre 1887 et 1914 à travers le journal de R. Viñes', *Revue internationale de musique française*, I/2 (1980), pp. 154–248

Haine, Malou, 'Cipa Godebski et les Apaches', *Revue belge de musicologie*, LX (2006), pp. 221–66
—, 'Cinq entretiens inédits de Jane Bathori avec Stéphane Audel', *Revue musicale de Suisse romande*, LXI/2 (June 2008), pp. 4–39
Howat, Roy, *The Art of French Piano Music: Debussy, Ravel, Fauré, Chabrier* (New Haven, CT, and London, 2009)
—, 'Le *Trio* de Ravel cent ans après', *Cahiers Maurice Ravel*, XVII (2014–15), pp. 60–80
Kaminsky, Peter, ed., *Unmasking Ravel: New Perspectives on the Music* (Rochester, NY, 2011)
Kelly, Barbara, *Music and Ultramodernism in France: A Fragile Consensus, 1913–1939* (Woodbridge, 2013)
Kilpatrick, Emily, *The Operas of Maurice Ravel* (Cambridge, 2015)
—, 'Ravel's *Trois poèmes de Stéphane Mallarmé*: A Philosophy of Composition', *Music & Letters*, CI/3 (2020), pp. 532–9
—, *French Art Song: History of a New Music* (Rochester, NY, 2022)
Lawson, Rex, 'Maurice Ravel: *Frontispice* for Pianola', *Pianola Journal*, II (1989), pp. 35–8
Lechevalier, Bernard, Bernard Mercier and Fausto Viader, *Le Cerveau de Ravel* (Paris, 2023)
Long, Marguerite, *Au Piano avec Maurice Ravel* (Paris, 1971)
Marnat, Marcel, *Maurice Ravel* (Paris, 1986)
Mawer, Deborah, *The Ballets of Maurice Ravel: Creation and Interpretation* (Aldershot, 2006)
—, ed., *The Cambridge Companion to Ravel* (Cambridge, 2000)
—, ed., *Ravel Studies* (Cambridge, 2010)
Messing, Scott, 'Polemic as History: The Case of Neoclassicism', *Journal of Musicology*, IX/4 (Autumn 1991), pp. 481–97
Morrison, Simon, 'The Origins of *Daphnis et Chloé* (1912)', *19th-Century Music*, XXVIII/1 (Summer 2004), pp. 50–76
Newbould, Brian, 'Ravel's Pantoum', *Musical Times*, CXVI/1585 (March 1975), pp. 228–31
Nichols, Roger, *From Berlioz to Boulez* (London, 2022)
—, ed., *Ravel Remembered* (London, 1987)
Orenstein, Arbie, 'Some Unpublished Music and Letters by Maurice Ravel', *Music Forum*, III (1973), pp. 291–334
—, *Ravel: Man and Musician* (New York, 1975, revd edn 1991)
Pasler, Jann, 'A Sociology of the Apaches: "Sacred Battalion" for *Pelléas*', in *Berlioz and Debussy: Sources, Contexts and Legacies*, ed. Barbara Kelly and Kerry Murphy (Aldershot, 2007), pp. 149–66

Pichois, Claude, *Colette* (Paris, 1998)
Puri, Michael, *Ravel the Decadent: Memory, Sublimation and Desire* (New York, 2012)
Roberts, Paul, *Reflections: The Piano Music of Maurice Ravel* (Milwaukee, WI, 2012)
Roland-Manuel, *Maurice Ravel et son œuvre* (Paris, 1914)
—, 'Maurice Ravel', *La Revue musicale*, II/6 (April 1921), pp. 1–21
—, 'Maurice Ravel ou l'esthétique de l'imposture', *La Revue musicale*, VI/6 ('Maurice Ravel', April 1925), pp. 16–21
—, *Maurice Ravel et son œuvre dramatique* (Paris, 1928)
Rousseau-Plotto, Étienne, *Ravel: Portraits basques* (Anglet, 2004)
Saint-Marceaux, Marguerite de, *Journal, 1894–1927*, ed. Myriam Chimènes (Paris, 2007)
Trezise, Simon, ed., *The Cambridge Companion to French Music* (Cambridge, 2015)
Zank, Stephen, *Maurice Ravel: A Guide to Research* (New York, 2005)
—, *Irony and Sound: The Music of Maurice Ravel* (Rochester, NY, 2009)
Zwang, Gérard, *Mémoires d'une chanteuse française: La Vie et les amours de Madeleine Grey (1896–1979)* (Paris, 2008)

Acknowledgements

In early 2004, I wrote to the Fondation Maurice Ravel in Montfort-l'Amaury to ask whether there might be any work an Australian backpacker with high-school French could usefully undertake at the Musée Ravel. The response came with a rapidity and generosity that changed my life. Yes, I was welcome to come to Montfort. Le Belvédère had been closed for major repairs but was soon to reopen; assistance in the final stages of the restoration would be welcome, and some friends of the Fondation would be delighted to host me for the summer.

I came to know Ravel, then, by scrubbing his floors, sliding his books back on to their shelves, arranging his teacups on a tray, his glasses on their stand, his shaving mirror on the washstand and his chamber pot under the bed. I learned *Miroirs* at his piano and walked in the forest of Rambouillet. I sat on his balcony and talked to visitors, neighbours and some of the older *montfortois*, who could just remember, as children, calling 'Bonjour, Monsieur Ravel!' when they saw him working in his garden.

I will always be grateful to the late Arnaud and Henriette de Vitry, who welcomed me into their home that summer, and above all to the inimitable Claude Moreau, who worked for three decades as curator and guide at the Musée Ravel, and who became a beloved friend. 'Salut, petit Maurice!' Claude would call every morning, as she unlocked the doors and opened the shutters ('I need to let him know we're here'). Claude passed away a few days before I sat down to write these Acknowledgements. I offer this book to her memory in the hope that it might bring something of Ravel to life for its readers, as she brought him to life for me.

I am grateful for the collegiality of the international community of Ravel scholars, and thank, in particular, Roger Nichols, Arbie Orenstein and Manuel Cornejo for many sources and insights generously shared.

I acknowledge the institutional support of the Royal Academy of Music, and the endlessly helpful librarians of the Bibliothèque nationale de France. Above all, I offer loving thanks to Roy, and to Rosie and Felix.

Photo Acknowledgements

The author and publishers wish to express their thanks to the sources listed below for illustrative material and/or permission to reproduce it. Some locations of works are also given below, in the interest of brevity:

Bibliothèque historique de la Ville de Paris, photo Emily Kilpatrick: p. 70; Bibliothèque nationale de France, Paris: pp. 6, 9, 14, 17, 20, 24, 26, 49, 53, 56, 65, 75, 81, 87, 94, 104, 109, 124, 131, 141, 146, 152, 155, 163, 167; © Coll. Roland-Manuel: pp. 96 (photo Bibliothèque nationale de France, Paris), 128 (photo Diaph16/Benoît Musslin/Les Amis de Maurice Ravel); Conservatoire & Orchestre de Caen, Fonds Gabriel Dupont: p. 38; photos Institut national d'histoire de l'art (INHA), Paris (CC BY 4.0): pp. 79 (from *Musica*, 93 (June 1910)), 98 (from *Musica*, 19 (April 1904)); from Hélène Jourdan-Morhange, *Ravel et nous* (Geneva, 1945): pp. 43 (photo Pierre Petit), 121; from *Maurice Ravel par quelques-uns de ses familiers* (Paris, 1939): p. 22; The Morgan Library & Museum, New York: p. 113; Österreichische Nationalbibliothek, Vienna: p. 150; from *Revue musicale*, XIX/187 (December 1938): p. 148.